As of May 17, 2012, this guidance applies to federal savings associations in addition to national banks*

EP-LBS

Comptroller of the Currency
Administrator of National Banks

I0448219

Large Bank Supervision

Comptroller's Handbook

January 2010

EP

Bank Supervision and Examination Process

Contents

Introduction

Background

This booklet explains the philosophy and methods of the Office of the Comptroller of the Currency (OCC) for supervising the largest and most complex national banks. These banks include large banks as designated by the Senior Deputy Comptroller for Large Bank Supervision in Washington, D.C. and may include midsize banks at the discretion of the Deputy Comptroller for Midsize and Credit Card Banks. This guidance also pertains to foreign-owned U.S. branches and agencies, and international operations of both midsize and large banks.[1] When reviewing the international operations of national banks, examiners should also be guided by the Basel Committee's "Core Principles for Effective Banking Supervision."[2]

Many national banks are a part of diversified financial organizations. The OCC's large bank supervision program assesses the risks to the bank posed by related entities. This approach recognizes that risks present in a national bank may be mitigated or increased by activities in an affiliate.

Because of the vast — and in some cases global — operating scope of large banks, the OCC assigns examiners to work full-time at the largest institutions. This enables the OCC to maintain an ongoing program of risk assessment, monitoring, and communications with bank management and directors. Personnel selected for these assignments are rotated periodically to ensure that their supervisory perspective remains objective.

The OCC's large bank supervision objectives are designed to

- Determine the condition of the bank and the risks associated with current and planned activities, including relevant risks originating in subsidiaries and affiliates.
- Evaluate the overall integrity and effectiveness of risk management systems, using periodic validation through transaction testing.
- Determine compliance with laws and regulations.
- Communicate findings, recommendations, and requirements to bank management and directors in a clear and timely manner, and obtain informal or formal commitments to correct significant deficiencies.
- Verify the effectiveness of corrective actions, or, if actions have not been undertaken or accomplished, pursue timely resolution through more aggressive supervision or enforcement actions.

---

[1] More detailed guidance on the supervisory process for OCC-licensed offices of foreign banks can be found in the "Federal Branches and Agencies Supervision" booklet of the *Comptroller's Handbook*.
[2] The Basel Committee on Banking Supervision is a committee of banking supervisory authorities established by the central bank governors of the Group of Ten countries in 1975. The committee issued the "Core Principles for Effective Banking Supervision" in September 1997 and updated it in October 2006. The 25 principles establish minimum standards and are designed to promote more consistent and effective bank supervision in all countries.

In addition to performing their own analyses, the OCC's large bank examiners leverage the work of other OCC experts, other regulatory agencies, and outside auditors and analysts to supervise the bank. As the size and complexity of a bank's operations increase, so too does the need for close coordination among all relevant regulators. For banks with international operations or banks owned by foreign banking organizations, this includes coordination with foreign supervisors, as appropriate.

The foundation of large bank supervision is a risk assessment framework designed to determine that banks effectively assess risks throughout their entire enterprise, regardless of size, diversity of operations, or the existence of subsidiaries and affiliates. The risk assessment framework for large banks consists of the following three components:

- **Core Knowledge** — information in the OCC's supervisory information systems about an institution, its culture, risk profile, and other internal and external factors. This information enables examiners to communicate critical data to each other with greater consistency and efficiency.

- **Core Assessment** — standards and procedures that guide examiners in reaching conclusions on both risk assessments and regulatory ratings. Core assessment standards define the minimum conclusions that examiners must reach during every supervisory cycle to meet the requirements of a full-scope, on-site examination. The core assessment guidance in this booklet and the core examination procedures of the FFIEC *Bank Secrecy Act/Anti-Money Laundering (BSA/AML) Examination Manual* apply to all large banks, regardless of size or complexity. The guidance in this booklet and the core examination procedures of the FFIEC *Bank Secrecy Act/Anti-Money Laundering (BSA/AML) Examination Manual* apply to all large banks, regardless of size or complexity. The guidance permits examiners the flexibility and discretion to develop supervisory strategies that respond to existing and emerging risks.

- **Expanded Procedures** — detailed guidance that explains how to examine specialized activities or specific products that warrant extra attention beyond the core assessment. These procedures are found in other booklets of the *Comptroller's Handbook*, the FFIEC *Information Technology (IT) Examination Handbook*, and the FFIEC *BSA/AML Examination Manual*. Examiners determine which expanded procedures to use, if any, during examination planning, or after drawing preliminary conclusions during the core assessment.

Supervision by Risk

The OCC recognizes that banking is a business of assuming risks in order to earn profits. While banking risks historically have been concentrated in traditional banking activities, the financial services industry has evolved in response to market-driven, technological, and legislative changes. These changes have allowed banks to expand product offerings, geographic diversity, and delivery systems. They have also increased the complexity of the bank's consolidated risk exposure. Because of this complexity, banks must evaluate, control, and manage risk according to its significance. The bank's evaluation of risk must take into account how nonbank activities within a banking organization affect the bank. Consolidated risk assessments should be a fundamental part of managing the bank.

Large banks assume varied and complex risks that warrant a risk-oriented supervisory approach. Under this approach, examiners do not attempt to restrict risk-taking but rather determine whether banks identify and effectively manage the risks they assume. As an organization grows more diverse and complex, its risk management processes must keep pace. When risk is not properly managed, the OCC directs bank management to take corrective action. In all cases, the OCC's primary concern is that the bank operates in a safe and sound manner and maintains capital commensurate with its risk.

Supervision by risk allocates greater resources to areas with higher risks. The OCC accomplishes this by

- Identifying risks using common definitions. The categories of risk, as they are defined, are the foundation for supervisory activities.

- Measuring risks using common methods of evaluation. Risk cannot always be quantified in dollars. For example, adverse media coverage may indicate excessive reputation risk.

- Evaluating risk management to determine whether bank systems and processes permit management to adequately identify, measure, monitor, and control existing and prospective levels of risk.

Examiners should discuss preliminary conclusions regarding their assessment of risks with bank management. Following these discussions, they should adjust conclusions when appropriate. Once the risks have been clearly identified and communicated, the OCC can then focus supervisory efforts on the areas of greater risk within the bank, the consolidated banking company, and the banking system.

To fully implement supervision by risk, examiners must consider the risk profiles and assign regulatory ratings to the lead national bank and all affiliated national banks. Examiners may determine that risks in individual institutions are increased, reduced, or mitigated in light of the consolidated risk profile of the company as a whole. To perform a consolidated analysis, an examiner should obtain pertinent information from banks and affiliates (within the confines of the Gramm-Leach-Bliley Act of 1999, or GLBA), verify transactions flowing between banks and affiliates, and obtain information from other regulatory agencies, as necessary.

Banking Risks

From a supervisory perspective, risk is the potential that events, expected or unexpected, will have an adverse effect on a bank's earnings, capital, or franchise or enterprise value.[3] The OCC has defined eight categories of risk for bank supervision purposes: *credit, interest rate, liquidity, price, operational, compliance, strategic,* and *reputation.*[4] These categories are not mutually exclusive. Any product or service may expose a bank to multiple risks. Risks also may be interdependent and may be positively or negatively correlated. Examiners should be aware of this interdependence and assess the effect in a consistent and inclusive manner. Examiners also should be alert to concentrations that can significantly elevate risk. Concentrations can accumulate within and across products, business lines, geographic areas, countries, and legal entities. (Updated 5/06/2013)

The presence of risk is not necessarily reason for supervisory concern. Examiners determine whether the risks a bank assumes are warranted by assessing whether the risks are effectively managed, consistent with safe and sound banking practices. Generally, a risk is effectively managed when it is identified, understood, measured, monitored, and controlled as part of a deliberate risk/reward strategy, known as risk appetite. A bank should have the capacity to readily withstand the financial distress that such a risk, in isolation or in combination with other risks, could cause. (Updated 5/06/2013)

If examiners determine that a risk is unwarranted (i.e., not effectively managed or backed by adequate capital to support the activity), they must communicate to management and the board of directors the need to mitigate or eliminate the excessive risk. Appropriate actions may include reducing exposures, increasing capital, and strengthening risk management practices. (Updated 5/06/2013)

Risk Management

Because market conditions and company structures vary, no single risk management system works for all companies. The sophistication of risk management systems should be proportionate to the risks present and the size and complexity of an institution. As an organization grows more diverse and complex, the sophistication of its risk management must keep pace.

Risk management systems of large banks must be sufficiently comprehensive to enable senior management to identify and effectively manage the risk throughout the company. Examinations of large banks focus on the overall integrity and effectiveness of risk management systems. Periodic validation, a vital component of large bank examinations, verifies the integrity of these risk management systems.

---

[3] Enterprise value is an assessment of a bank's overall worth based on market perception of its ability to effectively manage operations and mitigate risk.

[4] The risk definitions are found in the "Risk Assessment System" section.

Sound risk management systems have several things in common; for example, they are independent of risk-taking activities. Regardless of the risk management system's design, each system should

- *Identify risk*: To properly identify risks, a bank must recognize and understand existing risks and risks that may arise from new business initiatives, including risks that originate in nonbank subsidiaries and affiliates, and those that arise from external market forces, or regulatory or statutory changes. Risk identification should be a continuing process, and should occur at both the transaction and portfolio level. A bank must also identify interdependencies and correlations across portfolios and lines of business that may amplify risk exposures. Proper risk identification is critical for banks undergoing mergers and consolidations to ensure that risks are appropriately addressed. Risk identification in merging companies begins with the establishment of uniform definitions of risk; a common language helps to ensure the merger's success.

- *Measure risk*: Accurate and timely measurement of risk is essential to effective risk management. A bank that does not have risk measurement tools has limited ability to control or monitor risk levels. Further, more sophisticated measurement tools are needed as the complexity of the risk increases. A bank should periodically test to make sure that the measurement tools it uses are accurate. Sound risk measurement tools assess the risks of individual transactions and portfolios, as well as interdependencies, correlations, and aggregate risks across portfolios and lines of business. During bank mergers and consolidations, the effectiveness of risk measurement tools is often impaired because of the technological incompatibility of the merging systems or other problems of integration. Consequently, the resulting company must make a concerted effort to ensure that risks are appropriately measured across the consolidated entity. Larger, more complex companies must assess the effect of increased transaction volume across all risk categories.

- *Monitor risk*: Banks should monitor risk levels to ensure timely review of risk positions and exceptions. Monitoring reports should be timely, accurate, and informative and should be distributed to appropriate individuals to ensure action, when needed. For large, complex companies, monitoring is essential to ensure that management's decisions are implemented for all geographies, products, and legal entities.

- *Control risk*: Banks should establish and communicate risk limits through policies, standards, and procedures that define responsibility and authority. These limits should serve as a means to control exposures to the various risks associated with the bank's activities. The limits should be tools that management can adjust when conditions or risk tolerances change. Banks should also have a process to authorize and document exceptions or changes to risk limits when warranted. In banks merging or consolidating, the transition should be tightly controlled; business plans, lines of authority, and accountability should be clear. Large, diversified companies should have strong risk controls covering all geographies, products, and legal entities to prevent undue concentrations of risk.

Board and Management Responsibilities

The board must establish the company's strategic direction and risk tolerances. In carrying out these responsibilities, the board should approve policies that set operational standards and risk limits. Well-designed monitoring systems will allow the board to hold management accountable for operating within established tolerances.

Capable management and appropriate staffing are essential to effective risk management. Bank management is responsible for the implementation, integrity, and maintenance of risk management systems. Management must

- Keep directors adequately informed about risk-taking activities.

- Implement the company's strategy.

- Develop policies that define the institution's risk tolerance and ensure that they are compatible with strategic goals.

- Ensure that strategic direction and risk tolerances are effectively communicated and adhered to throughout the organization.

- Oversee the development and maintenance of management information systems to ensure that information is timely, accurate, and pertinent.

Risk Management Assessment Factors

When examiners assess risk management systems, they consider the bank's policies, processes, personnel, and control systems. If any of these areas is deficient, so is the bank's risk management.

Policies are statements of actions adopted by a bank to pursue certain objectives. Policies often set standards (on risk tolerances, for example) and should be consistent with the bank's underlying mission, values, and principles. A policy review should always be triggered when the bank's objectives or standards change. (Updated 5/06/2013)

Processes are the procedures, programs, and practices that impose order on a bank's pursuit of its objectives. Processes define how daily activities are carried out. Effective processes are consistent with the underlying policies and are governed by appropriate checks and balances (such as internal controls). (Updated 5/06/2013)

Personnel are the bank staff and managers who execute or oversee processes. Personnel should be qualified and competent, and should perform appropriately. They should understand the bank's mission, values, principles, policies, and processes. Banks should design compensation programs to attract, develop, and retain qualified personnel. In addition, compensation programs should be structured in a manner that encourages strong risk management practices. (Updated 5/06/2013)

Control systems are the functions (such as internal and external audits, risk review, and quality assurance) and information systems that bank managers use to measure performance, make decisions about risk, and assess the effectiveness of processes. Control functions should have clear reporting lines, adequate resources, and appropriate authority. Management information systems should provide timely, accurate, and relevant feedback. (Updated 5/06/2013)

Measuring and Assessing Risk

Using the OCC's core assessment standards[5] as a guide, an examiner obtains both a current and prospective view of a bank's risk profile and determines its overall condition. When appropriate, this risk profile incorporates the potential material risks to the bank from functionally regulated activities conducted by the bank or the bank's functionally regulated affiliates (FRAs).[6]

The core assessment provides the conclusions to complete the OCC's risk assessment system (RAS). Examiners document their conclusions regarding the quantity of risk, the quality of risk management, the level of supervisory concern (measured as aggregate risk), and the direction of risk using the RAS. Together, the core assessment and the RAS enable the OCC to measure and assess existing and emerging risks in large banks, regardless of their size or complexity. This risk assessment drives supervisory strategies and activities. It also facilitates discussions with bank management and directors and helps to ensure more efficient examinations.

Core Assessment

The core assessment establishes the minimum conclusions examiners must reach to evaluate risks and assign regulatory ratings. Examiners complete the core assessment summary for each consolidated company during every supervisory cycle.[7] The EIC or supervisory office can perform the core assessment (or portions of it) more often, if deemed appropriate.

The standards are sufficiently flexible to be applied to all companies; examiners can use the standards to assess risks for all product lines and legal entities. The consistent structure of the core assessment facilitates the analysis of risk in merging companies because examiners use a common language and the same standards to assess risks.

When using the core assessment standards, examiners should use judgment in deciding how to perform their assessments and the level of independent testing needed. Examiners should be alert to specific activities or risks that may trigger the need for the EIC to broaden the scope of the examination. Examiners can expand the examination procedures to include procedures from other *Comptroller's Handbook* booklets, such as "Loan Portfolio

---

[5] The core assessment standards are detailed in the "Core Assessment" section.
[6] Refer to the Functional Regulation section of the "Bank Supervision Process" booklet.
[7] Completion of the core assessment should generally result in the issuance of reports of examination (ROEs) to the lead national bank and each affiliated national bank.

Management," "Liquidity," and "Country Risk Management." Any decision to modify the scope of an examination should be documented in the appropriate OCC supervisory information system.

Examiners should also use judgment in the level of documentation needed to support the core assessment. The core assessment consists of assessment factors and sub-factors for each risk. Normally, there is no need for examiners to document every sub-factor under each assessment factor. However, the level of documentation should be commensurate with the risks facing the institution. The level of documentation may vary over time depending on changes in the company's condition, its risk profile, pending or actual enforcement actions, violations of law, or referrals to other agencies.

Risk Assessment System

By completing the core assessment and, as necessary, expanded procedures, examiners can assess the risk exposure for the eight categories of risk using the RAS. For six of the eight risks — *credit, interest rate, liquidity, price, operational,* and *compliance* — the supervisory process identifies

- **Quantity of risk** — the level or volume of risk that exists; characterized as high, moderate, or low.

- **Quality of risk management** — how well risks are identified, measured, controlled, and monitored; characterized as strong, satisfactory, or weak.

- **Aggregate risk** — the level of supervisory concern, which is a summary judgment incorporating the assessments of the quantity of risk and the quality of risk management (examiners weigh the relative importance of each). Aggregate risk is characterized as high, moderate, or low.

- **Direction of risk** — a prospective assessment of the probable movement in aggregate risk over the next 12 months; characterized as decreasing, stable, or increasing. The direction of risk often influences the supervisory strategy, including how much validation is needed. If risk is decreasing, the examiner expects, based on current information, aggregate risk to decline over the next 12 months. If risk is stable, the examiner expects aggregate risk to remain unchanged. If risk is increasing, the examiner expects aggregate risk to be higher in 12 months.

Because an examiner expects aggregate risk to increase or decrease does not necessarily mean that he or she expects the movement to be sufficient to change the aggregate risk level within 12 months. An examiner can expect movement **within** the risk level. For example, aggregate risk can be high and decreasing even though the decline is not anticipated to change the level of aggregate risk to moderate. In such circumstances, examiners should explain in narrative comments why a change in the risk level is not expected. Aggregate risk assessments of high and increasing or low and decreasing are possible.

When assessing direction of risk, examiners should consider current practices and activities in addition to other quantitative and qualitative factors. For example, the direction of credit risk may be increasing if a bank has relaxed underwriting standards during a strong economic cycle, even though the volume of troubled credits and credit losses remains low. Similarly, the direction of liquidity risk may be increasing if a bank has not implemented a well-developed contingency funding plan during a strong economic cycle, even though existing liquidity sources are sufficient for current conditions.

Although the two remaining risks — *strategic* and *reputation* — affect an institution's franchise or enterprise value, they are difficult to measure precisely. Consequently, the OCC assesses only the **aggregate risk** and **direction of risk** for these two risks. The characterizations of aggregate risk and direction of risk are the same as for the other six risks.

As the primary regulator of national banks, the OCC has the responsibility for evaluating the overall or *consolidated* risk profile of such banks. The consolidated risk profile is developed by combining the assessment of risks at each affiliated national bank, including an assessment of the material risks posed to the bank or the company by the bank's or any FRA's functionally regulated activities, as appropriate. The relative importance of each risk, both for an individual bank and for the consolidated company, should influence the development of the supervisory strategy and the assignment of resources.

Examiners complete a RAS summary for the *consolidated* company quarterly, or more often if its risk profile or condition warrants. One of these quarterly assessments accompanies the annual core assessment and includes a comprehensive narrative on the aggregate risk, direction of risk, and when applicable, quantity of risk and quality of risk management, for each risk category. The three remaining quarterly assessments update the annual assessment and serve to highlight any changes in the company's or an individual bank's risk profile. The EIC and the supervisory office will determine the appropriate form and extent of any supporting narratives that accompany these intervening updates. Examiners record the quarterly risk assessments in the OCC's supervisory information systems.

Examiners should discuss their conclusions with appropriate management and the board. Bank management may provide information that helps the examiner clarify or modify his or her conclusions. Following the discussions, the OCC and company management should have a common understanding of the bank's risks, the strengths and weaknesses of its risk management, management's commitment and action plans to address any weaknesses, and future OCC supervisory plans.

Internal Control and Audit

Examiners evaluate and validate the two fundamental components of any bank's risk management system — internal control and audit — as part of the core assessment. An accurate evaluation of internal control and audit is crucial to the proper supervision of a bank. Examiners communicate to the bank their overall assessments (strong, satisfactory, or weak) of the system of internal control and the audit program, along with any significant concerns or weaknesses, in the report of examination. Based on these assessments, examiners determine the amount of reliance they can place on internal control and audit for areas under examination. Effective internal control and audit help to leverage OCC resources and establish the scope of current and planned supervisory activities.

Internal Control

An effective system of internal control is the backbone of a bank's risk management system. As required in 12 CFR 363, bank management must assess the effectiveness of the bank's internal control structure annually and the external auditors must attest to management's assertions.[8] Examiners should obtain an understanding of how the auditors reached their conclusions for their attestation of management's assertions.

The core assessment includes factors for assessing a bank's control environment during each supervisory cycle. The factors are consistent with industry-accepted criteria[9] for establishing and evaluating the effectiveness of internal control. When examiners need to use expanded procedures, they should refer to the "Internal Control" or other appropriate booklets of the *Comptroller's Handbook*, the FFIEC *IT Examination Handbook*, or the FFIEC *BSA/AML Examination Manual*. These resources provide more information on the types of internal controls commonly used in specific banking functions.

Audit

The EIC, in consultation with the supervisory office, tailors the scope of the audit assessment to the bank's size, activities, and risk profile. Examiners assigned to review audit, through coordination and integration with examiners reviewing other functional and specialty areas, determine how much reliance can be placed on the audit program by validating the adequacy of the audit's scope and effectiveness during each supervisory cycle.

Validation, which encompasses observation, inquiry, and testing, generally consists of a combination of discussions with bank/audit management or personnel and reviews of audit work papers and processes (e.g., policy adherence, risk assessments, follow-up activities). Examiners use the following three successive steps, as needed, to validate the audit program:

- Review of internal audit work papers.
- Expanded procedures.
- Verification procedures.

---

[8] National banks that are subject to 12 CFR 363 or that file periodic reports under 12 CFR 11 and 12 CFR 16.20 may be subject to the provisions of the Sarbanes-Oxley Act. For more information, refer to the "Internal and External Audits" booklet of the *Comptroller's Handbook*.

[9] The Committee of Sponsoring Organizations of the Treadway Commission (COSO) 1992 report "Internal Control — Integrated Framework" discusses control system structures and components. COSO is a voluntary private-sector organization, formed in 1985, dedicated to improving the quality of financial reporting through business ethics, effective internal control, and corporate governance. COSO was jointly sponsored by the American Accounting Association, the American Institute of Certified Public Accountants, the Financial Executives Institute, the Institute of Internal Auditors, and the National Association of Accountants.

The review of internal audit work papers, including those from outsourced internal audit, may not be waived during any supervisory cycle. However, the EIC has flexibility in limiting the scope of the work paper reviews (i.e., the number of internal audit programs or work papers reviewed) based on his or her familiarity with the bank's audit function and findings from the previous review of internal audit. Examiners typically do not review external audit work papers[10] unless the review of the internal audit function discloses significant issues (e.g., insufficient audit coverage) or questions are raised about matters normally within the scope of an external audit program.

Examiners may identify significant audit or control discrepancies or weaknesses, or may raise questions about the audit function's effectiveness after completing the core assessment. In those situations, examiners should consider expanding the scope of the review by selecting expanded procedures in the "Internal and External Audits," "Internal Control," or other appropriate booklets of the *Comptroller's Handbook*, the FFIEC *IT Examination Handbook*, or the FFIEC *BSA/AML Examination Manual*.

When reviewing the audit function, significant concerns may remain about the adequacy or independence of an audit or internal control or about the integrity of a bank's financial or risk management controls. If so, examiners should consider further expanding the audit review to include verification procedures. Even when the external auditor issues an unqualified opinion, verification procedures should be considered if discrepancies or weaknesses call into question the accuracy of the opinion. The extent to which examiners perform verification procedures will be decided on a case-by-case basis after consultation with the supervisory office.[11] Direct confirmation with the bank's customers must have prior approval of the appropriate deputy comptroller. The Enforcement and Compliance Division should also be notified when direct confirmations are being considered.

If examiners identify significant audit weaknesses, the EIC will recommend to the appropriate supervisory office what formal or informal action is needed to ensure timely corrective measures. Consideration should be given to whether the bank complies with the laws and regulations[12] that establish minimum requirements for internal and external audit programs. Further, if the bank does not meet the audit system operational and managerial standards of 12 CFR 30, appendix A, possible options to consider are having bank management develop a compliance plan, consistent with 12 CFR 30, to address the weaknesses, or making the bank subject to other types of enforcement actions. In making a decision, the supervisory office will consider the significance of the weaknesses, the overall audit assessment, audit-related matters requiring attention (MRA), management's ability and commitment to effect corrective action, and the risks posed to the bank.

---

[10] Prior to reviewing external auditor work papers, examiners should meet with bank management and the external auditor, consult with the OCC's chief accountant, and obtain approval from the supervisory office.

[11] Internal control questionnaires (ICQs) and verification procedures can be found on Examiner's Library and the *e files* DVDs.

[12] For more information on the laws, regulations, and policy guidance relating to internal and external audit programs, refer to the "Internal and External Audits" booklet of the *Comptroller's Handbook*.

The Supervisory Process

The OCC fulfills its mission principally through its program to supervise national banks on an ongoing basis. Supervision is more than just on-site activities that result in an examination report. It includes discovery of a bank's condition, ensuring correction of significant deficiencies, and monitoring the bank's activities and progress. In large banks, examination activities occur throughout the supervisory cycle. Regardless of the size or complexity of the bank, all OCC examination activities depend on careful planning, effective management throughout the supervisory cycle, and clear communication of results to bank management and the board.

Planning

Planning is essential to effective supervision. During planning, examiners develop detailed strategies for providing effective, efficient supervision to each bank and company. Planning requires careful and thoughtful assessment of a bank's current and anticipated risks. In other words, examiners should assess the risks of both existing and new banking activities. New banking activities may be either traditional activities that are new to the bank or activities new to the financial services industry.[13] The supervisory strategy should also incorporate an assessment of the company's merger and acquisition plans and any conditions attached to corporate decisions.

Effective planning for all large companies, especially complex, diversified firms, requires adequate and timely communication among supervisory agencies, including functional regulators. Effective functional supervision is attained through close cooperation and coordination among the various regulators. EICs should maintain open channels of communication with other regulators and work directly with them on institution-specific items. By doing so, EICs help promote comprehensive supervision and reduce the burden of overlapping jurisdiction on the regulated entities. Interagency guidelines on coordination among U.S. banking regulators are detailed in Banking Bulletin 93-38. Examiners should comply with all other formalized agreements among regulators to ensure that intracompany supervision is comprehensive and consistent.

Examiners planning supervisory activities of international operations should also coordinate with the International Banking Supervision division regarding communications with foreign bank supervisors.[14]

Planning also requires effective and periodic communication with bank management. Supervisory strategies are dynamic documents reviewed and updated frequently based on company, industry, economic, legislative, and regulatory developments. Examiners should discuss supervisory strategies with bank management as the plans are made and when any of the plans are modified.

---

[13] Refer to OCC Bulletin 2004-20, "Risk Management of New, Expanded, or Modified Bank Products and Services."

[14] Examiners can refer to PPM 5500-1 (Revised), "Coordination with Foreign Supervisors."

EICs develop consolidated supervisory strategies for each company. The appropriate supervisory deputy comptroller reviews and approves them. If necessary, consolidated strategies can be supplemented by plans specific to one or more affiliates. Examiners document strategies for each company in the appropriate OCC supervisory information system.

Examination activities are based on supervisory strategies. The strategies should focus examiners' efforts on monitoring the effectiveness of the bank's risk management processes and seeking bank management's commitment to correct previously identified deficiencies. When possible, supervisory activities should rely on the bank's internal systems, including its internal and external audit activities and risk management systems, to assess the condition and the extent of risks. These systems must be periodically tested and validated for integrity and reliability during the course of routine supervisory activities.

Each supervisory strategy is based on

- The **core knowledge** of the bank, including its
  - Risk profile.
  - Regulatory ratings.
  - Management.
  - Control environment.
  - Audit program.
  - Compliance risk management system.
  - Market(s).
  - Products and activities.
  - Information technology support and services.

- OCC supervisory guidance and other factors, including
  - Supervisory history.
  - Core assessment.
  - Other examination guidelines (e.g., expanded procedures in the *Comptroller's Handbook*, the FFIEC *IT Examination Handbook*, and the FFIEC *BSA/AML Examination Manual*).
  - Supervisory priorities of the agency that may arise from time to time.
  - Applicable economic conditions.

- Statutory examination requirements.[15]

Elements of a Supervisory Strategy

Supervisory strategies are comprised of objectives, activities, and work plans. An effective supervisory strategy for large banks generally will include

---

[15] Information on the statutory requirements for examinations can be found in the "Bank Supervision Process" booklet of the *Comptroller's Handbook*.

- The supervisory objectives for the year.
- An identification of the ongoing bank supervisory activities and the targeted examinations recommended for each quarter of the year. This information is often consolidated by each RAS element included on the OCC's quarterly risk assessment and then modified to address the bank's specific risk profile, including areas of potential or actual risk, emerging risks, and regulatory mandated examination areas.
- An indication of the complexity, workdays, and expertise of staff needed to perform the bank supervisory activities recommended for the year.
- A preliminary budget projection of the work to be completed, including any international travel.
- An internal and external communications strategy for the year. This communications strategy details the types of information examiners will exchange with boards of directors, bank management and staff, and other regulators and describes how this information will be exchanged (i.e., meetings, reports). The communications strategy will also describe what information about the bank will be produced and shared internally with OCC management and staff.
- An overview of the profiles of the significant lines of business (optional).

The strategies are prepared by the EIC and resident staff of each institution and approved by the large bank deputy comptrollers. These strategies are updated throughout the year based on changing risks to national banks and the banking system, conflicting resource demands, system conversions, and changes in supervisory priorities. Updates to supervisory strategies are documented in the appropriate OCC supervisory information system.

Examining

Examining involves discovering a bank's condition, ensuring that the bank corrects significant deficiencies, and monitoring ongoing activities. When assessing the bank's condition, examiners must consider the risk associated with activities performed by the bank and its nonbank subsidiaries and affiliates. Examiners must meet certain minimum objectives during the supervisory cycle, which are defined in the core assessment and include the core examination procedures in the FFIEC *BSA/AML Examination Manual*. Examiners must also assess the overall risk and assign or confirm the CAMELS composite and component ratings, the information technology (IT) rating, the asset management rating, and the consumer compliance rating. Community Reinvestment Act (CRA) examinations for banks with assets in excess of $250 million are ordinarily conducted within 36 months from the close of the prior CRA examination, depending upon the bank's risk characteristics.[16]

In large banks, examiners perform their work throughout the supervisory cycle through various ongoing supervisory activities or targeted examinations. Targeted examinations are often conducted as integrated risk reviews by business or product line. Since a product may have implications for several risk categories, the targeted reviews evaluate risk controls and

---

[16] Further information regarding CRA examinations can be found in the "Community Reinvestment Act Examination Procedures" booklet of the *Comptroller's Handbook* and OCC Bulletins 2006-17 and 2000-35.

processes for each applicable risk category. For example, a targeted review of credit card lending activities evaluates credit risk; operational risk from credit card fraud, processing errors, or service interruptions; interest rate risk from low introductory rates; compliance risk from disclosure problems; and reputation risk from predatory lending practices or inadequate controls to ensure the confidentiality and privacy of consumer information. Findings from these targeted, integrated examinations provide input for the annual core assessment and quarterly RAS updates.

Discovery

Through discovery, examiners gain a fundamental understanding of the condition of the bank, the quality of management, and the effectiveness of risk management systems. This understanding helps examiners focus their supervision on the areas of greatest concern.

A primary objective of discovery is to validate the integrity of risk management systems. During the validation process, examiners should perform independent tests, in proportion to the risk they find. Examiners should periodically ensure that key control functions within a bank are validated. (Updated 5/06/2013)

In discovery, examiners

- Evaluate the bank's condition.
- Identify significant risks.
- Quantify the risk.
- Evaluate management's and the board's awareness and understanding of the significant risks.
- Assess the quality of risk management.
- Perform sufficient testing to validate the integrity of risk management systems, particularly audit and internal control. (Updated 5/06/2013)
- Identify unacceptable levels of risk, deficiencies in risk management systems, and the underlying causes of any deficiencies.

The examiner's evaluations and assessments form the foundation for future supervisory activities. Many of these assessments are part of the core knowledge of the institution. Bank supervision is an ongoing process that enables examiners to periodically confirm and update their assessments to reflect current or emerging risks. This revalidation is fundamental to effective supervision.

Correction

In the correction process, examiners seek bank management's commitment to correct significant deficiencies and verify that the bank's corrective actions have been successful and timely.

In correction, examiners

- Solicit commitments from management to correct each significant deficiency.
- Review bank-prepared action plans to resolve each significant deficiency, including the appropriateness of the time frames for correction.
- Verify that the bank is executing the action plans.
- Evaluate whether the actions the bank has taken (or plans to take) adequately address the deficiencies.
- Resolve open supervisory issues through informal or formal actions.

Examiners should ensure that bank management's efforts to correct deficiencies address *root causes* rather than symptoms. To do so, examiners may require management to develop new systems or improve the design and implementation of existing systems or processes.

The bank's plans for corrective actions should be formally communicated through action plans. Action plans detail steps or methods management has determined will correct the root causes of deficiencies. Bank management is responsible for developing and executing action plans. Directors are expected to hold management accountable for executing action plans.

Action plans should

- Specify actions to correct deficiencies.
- Address the underlying root causes of significant deficiencies.
- Set realistic time frames for completion.
- Establish benchmarks to measure progress toward completion.
- Identify the bank personnel who will be responsible for correction.
- Detail how the board and management will monitor actions and ensure effective execution of the plan.

The OCC's supervision of deficient areas focuses on verifying execution of the action plan and validating its success. When determining whether to take further action, examiners consider the responsiveness of the bank in recognizing the problem and formulating an effective solution. When the bank is unresponsive or unable to effect resolution, the OCC may take more formal steps to ensure correction.

Monitoring

Ongoing monitoring allows the OCC to respond promptly to risks facing individual banks and the industry as a whole. The dynamic nature of large banks makes this an important part of effective supervision.

In monitoring a bank, examiners

- Identify current and prospective issues that affect the bank's risk profile or overall condition.

- Determine how to focus future supervisory strategies.
- Measure the bank's progress in correcting deficiencies.
- Communicate with management regarding areas of concern, if any.

Monitoring activities are focused on assessing the bank's risks, including any potential material risks posed by functionally regulated activities conducted by the bank or FRAs. Activities are adjusted to include the risks facing each significant affiliated national bank. More complex institutions generally require more frequent and comprehensive oversight. In addition to assessing progress in executing plans and correcting deficiencies as needed, examiners are required to meet certain minimum requirements for monitoring activities for large banks.

On a quarterly basis, and generally within 45 days following the end of each quarter, examiners should

- Review and evaluate the company-prepared consolidated analysis of financial condition, including its significant operating units.

- Identify any significant issues that may result in changes to the CAMELS, IT, asset management, and consumer compliance ratings for the lead national bank and any affiliated national banks. If an issue is identified that affects a rating, the examiner must update the rating, assess the effect of the change on the risk profile, and adjust the supervisory strategy to reflect the change in condition. Note: A CRA examination must be performed to change a CRA rating.

- Update the *consolidated risk* profile of the company using the RAS summary. One of these quarterly assessments accompanies the annual core assessment and includes a comprehensive narrative on the aggregate risk, direction of risk, and when applicable, quantity of risk and quality of risk management, for each risk category. The three remaining quarterly assessments are used to update the annual assessment and serve to highlight any changes in the company's or an individual bank's risk profile.

- Review and update the supervisory strategy for the company and data in the OCC's supervisory information systems to ensure they are current and accurate. The EIC should change the strategies for individual banks if warranted. Examiners should discuss any significant changes with bank management and obtain approval from their supervisory office.

Communication

Communication is essential to high-quality bank supervision. The OCC is committed to ongoing, effective communication with the banks that it supervises and with other banking and functional regulators. Communication includes formal and informal conversations and meetings, examination reports, and other written materials. Regardless of form, communications should convey a consistent opinion of the bank's condition. All OCC communications must be professional, objective, clear, and informative.

Communication should be ongoing throughout the supervision process and must be tailored to a bank's structure and dynamics. The timing and form of communication depends on the situation being addressed. Examiners should communicate with the bank's management and board as often as the bank's condition and supervisory findings require. Examiners must include detailed plans for communication in the supervisory strategy for the bank or company.

By meeting with management often and directors as needed, examiners can ensure that all current issues are discussed. These meetings, which establish and maintain open lines of communication, are an important source of monitoring information. Examiners should document these meetings in the OCC's supervisory information systems.

Examiners must clearly and concisely communicate significant weaknesses or unwarranted risks to bank management, allowing management an opportunity to resolve differences, commit to corrective action, or correct the weakness. Examiners should describe the weaknesses, as well as the board's or management's commitment to corrective action, as "Matters Requiring Attention" (MRA) in the ROE or in other periodic written communications.[17]

Entrance or Planning Meetings with Management

The EIC will meet with appropriate bank or company management at the beginning of an examination to

- Explain the scope of the examination, the role of each examiner, and how the examination team will conduct the examination.
- Confirm the availability of bank personnel.
- Identify communication contacts.
- Answer any questions.

If an examination will be conducted jointly with another regulator, the OCC should invite a representative from that agency to participate in the entrance meeting.

Exit Meetings with Management

After each significant supervisory activity is completed, the EIC will meet with bank or company management to discuss findings, any significant issues, the areas of greatest risk to the bank, preliminary ratings, and plans for future supervisory activities. The EIC should encourage bankers to respond to OCC concerns, provide clarification, ask about future supervisory plans, and raise any other questions or concerns. At the exit meeting, the examiners will ask for management's commitment to correct weaknesses noted during the

---

[17] Refer to the "Bank Supervision Process" booklet, appendix I, for the definition of and guidance on Matters Requiring Attention.

supervisory activity and will, when appropriate, offer examples of acceptable solutions to identified problems.

In large or departmentalized banks, examiners may conduct exit meetings with management of specific departments or functions before the final exit meeting. The functional EICs summarize the issues and commitments for corrective actions from these meetings. The bank EIC then discusses them with senior bank management at the final exit meeting.

Before the exit meeting, the EIC should discuss significant findings, including preliminary ratings, with the appropriate OCC supervisory office. This discussion helps ensure that OCC policy is consistently applied and that OCC management supports the conclusions and any corrective action. The EIC and the supervisory office should also decide who will attend the exit meeting on behalf of the OCC, and inquire about the attendance of senior bank managers and others. If the examination was conducted jointly with another regulator, the supervisory office should invite a representative from that agency to participate in the exit meeting.

Examiners must ensure that any significant decisions discussed during the exit meeting are effectively conveyed in the meeting with the board and in written correspondence. Examiners should discuss all issues with management before discussing them with the board, unless, in the supervisory office's view, the subject is best approached confidentially with the board.

Written Communication

Written communication of supervisory activities and findings is essential to effective supervision. Examiners should periodically provide written communication to the board highlighting significant issues that arise during the supervisory process. This communication should focus the board's attention on the OCC's major conclusions, including any significant problems. This written record, along with other related correspondence, helps establish and support the OCC's supervisory strategy.

Written communication must

- Be consistent with the tone, findings, and conclusions orally communicated to the bank.
- Convey the condition of the bank or, if appropriate, the condition of an operational unit of the bank.
- Be addressed to the appropriate audience based on how the bank or company is structured and managed.
- Discuss any concerns the OCC has about bank risks, deficiencies in risk management, or significant violations.
- Summarize the actions and commitments that the OCC will require of the bank to correct deficiencies and violations.
- Be concise to ensure that the issues are clear.

In addition to written communication throughout a supervisory cycle, **the OCC must provide each national bank's board of directors a report of examination (ROE) at least once during every supervisory cycle.** The ROE conveys the overall condition and risk profile of the bank, and summarizes examination activities and findings during the supervisory cycle.[18] The ROE

- Contains conclusions on assigned ratings and the adequacy of the bank's BSA/AML compliance program.
- Discusses significant deficiencies, violations, and excessive risks.
- Details corrective action to which the board or management has committed.

Meetings with the Board of Directors

The OCC maintains communication with boards of directors throughout the supervisory cycle to discuss OCC examination results and other matters of mutual interest, including current industry issues, emerging industry risks, and legislative issues. The EIC will meet with the board of directors or an authorized committee that includes outside directors after the board or committee has reviewed the report of examination findings. If necessary, the OCC will use board meetings to discuss how the board should respond supervisory concerns and issues.

The OCC will conduct a board meeting at least once during every supervisory cycle for the lead national bank. More frequent meetings should be conducted when justified by the bank's condition or special supervisory needs. When meetings are routinely conducted with board committees, examiners are also encouraged to meet periodically with the full board to confirm findings and facilitate effective communication. Examiners should conduct board meetings with affiliated national banks that are not lead banks only when significant supervisory concerns exist or when meetings will enhance overall supervision.

The EIC conducting the meeting should be prepared to discuss methods of corrective action, as well as to discuss all findings, conclusions, and concerns. The EIC should encourage board members to ask questions or make comments. Senior management of the appropriate OCC supervisory office should attend and participate in board meetings with large banks. If the examination was conducted jointly with another regulator, the supervisory office should invite a representative from that agency to participate in the board meeting.

OCC's Supervisory Information Systems

Examiners record and communicate narrative and statistical information on institutions of supervisory interest to the OCC using the agency's supervisory information systems. These institutions include banks, holding companies and affiliates, federal branches and agencies of foreign banks, and independent technology service providers.

The recorded information will reflect the current condition, supervisory strategy, and supervisory concerns for each bank. It also documents follow-up actions, board meeting discussions, commitments to corrective action, progress in correcting identified problems,

---

[18] Refer to the "Bank Supervision Process" booklet, appendix I, for ROE content, structure, and review requirements.

and significant events. Using these electronic records, OCC senior management can review the condition of individual banks and groups of banks. Other federal banking regulators also have access to the information, as appropriate, through various formats.

Many electronic files are official records of the OCC and may be discoverable items in litigation. When writing electronic comments, examiners must be succinct, clear, and professional, avoiding any informality that might be misunderstood or misused.

The EIC and the supervisory office are responsible for ensuring that the electronic files for their assigned institutions are accurate and up-to-date.

Core Assessment

Examiners complete the core assessment for each consolidated company during every supervisory cycle.[19] Examiners should also periodically ensure that key control functions within a bank are validated. The core assessment summary should be documented in the OCC's supervisory information systems.

Strategic Risk

Examiners consider the following assessment factors when making judgments about strategic risk. These factors are the minimum **standards** that all examiners consider during every supervisory cycle to ensure quality supervision. Examiners are required to judge, based on the review of the core assessment factors, whether the risk is low, moderate, or high.

Strategic Factors

☐ Low	☐ Moderate	☐ High

- The magnitude of change in established corporate mission, goals, culture, values, or risk tolerance.
- The financial objectives as they relate to the short- and long-term goals of the bank.
- The market situation, including product, customer demographics, and geographic position.
- Diversification by product, geography, and customer demographics.
- Risk of implementing innovative or unproven products, services, or technologies.
- Merger and acquisition plans and opportunities.
- Potential or planned entrance into new businesses, product lines, or delivery channels, or implementation of new systems.
- The effect of cost control initiatives, if any.
- The influence of the ultimate parent, including foreign owners.

External Factors

☐ Low	☐ Moderate	☐ High

- The effect of economic, industry, and market conditions; legislative and regulatory change; technological advances; and competition.

Management, Processes, and Systems

☐ Low	☐ Moderate	☐ High

- The expertise of senior management and the effectiveness of the board of directors.

---

[19] Completion of the core assessment should generally result in the issuance of reports of examination (ROEs) to the lead national bank and each affiliated national bank.

- The priority and compatibility of personnel, technology, and capital resources allocation with strategic initiatives.
- The adequacy of the new product process.
- Past performance in offering new products or services and evaluating potential and consummated acquisitions.
- Performance in implementing new technology or systems.
- The effectiveness of management's methods of communicating, implementing, and modifying strategic plans, and consistency with stated risk tolerance and policies.
- The adequacy and independence of controls to monitor business decisions.
- The responsiveness to identified deficiencies in internal control and compliance systems.
- The quality, integrity, timeliness, and relevance of reports to the board of directors necessary to oversee strategic decisions.
- The ability to identify and manage fair lending, community reinvestment, BSA/AML/OFAC, and other compliance issues in conjunction with strategic initiatives.
- The appropriateness of performance management and compensation programs, including accountability for compliance with BSA/AML/OFAC, consumer protection, and other laws and regulations. Such programs should exclude incentives for personnel to take excessive risks. (Updated 9/28/2012)

Reputation Risk

Examiners consider the following assessment factors when making judgments about reputation risk. These factors are the minimum **standards** that all examiners consider during every supervisory cycle to ensure quality supervision. Examiners are required to judge, based on the review of the core assessment factors, whether the risk is low, moderate, or high.

Strategic Factors

☐ Low	☐ Moderate	☐ High

- The volume and types of assets and number of accounts under management or administration.
- Merger and acquisition plans and opportunities.
- Potential or planned entrance into new businesses, product lines, or technologies (including new delivery channels), particularly those that may test legal boundaries.

External Factors

☐ Low	☐ Moderate	☐ High

- The market's or public's perception of the corporate citizenship, mission, culture, and risk tolerance of the bank.
- The market's or public's perception of the bank's financial stability.
- The market's or public's perception of the quality of products and services offered by the bank.
- The effect of economic, industry, and market conditions; legislative and regulatory change; technological advances; and competition.

Management, Processes, and Systems

☐ Low	☐ Moderate	☐ High

- Past performance in offering new products or services and in conducting due diligence prior to startup.
- Past performance in developing or implementing new technologies and systems.
- The nature of, amount of, and ability to minimize exposure from litigation, monetary penalties, violations of laws and regulations, and customer complaints.
- The expertise of senior management and the effectiveness of the board of directors in maintaining an ethical, self-policing culture.
- Management's willingness and ability to adjust strategies based on regulatory changes, market disruptions, market or public perception, and legal losses.
- The quality and integrity of management information systems and the development of expanded or newly integrated systems.
- The adequacy and independence of controls used to monitor business decisions.
- The responsiveness to deficiencies in internal control and compliance risk management systems, including BSA/AML/OFAC-related systems. (Updated 9/28/2012)

- The ability to communicate effectively with the market, public, and media.
- Policies, practices, and systems protecting information consumers might consider private or confidential from deliberate or accidental disclosure.
- Management's responsiveness to internal, external, and regulatory review findings.
- The appropriateness of performance management and compensation programs, including accountability for compliance with BSA/AML/OFAC, consumer protection, and other laws and regulations. Such programs should exclude incentives for personnel to take excessive risks. (Updated 9/28/2012)

Credit Risk

Quantity of Credit Risk

Examiners consider the following assessment factors when making judgments about the quantity of credit risk. These factors are the minimum **standards** that all examiners consider during every supervisory cycle to ensure quality supervision. Examiners should apply the standards consistent with the guidelines in the "Loan Portfolio Management" booklet of the *Comptroller's Handbook*. Examiners are required to judge, based on the review of the core assessment factors, whether the risk is low, moderate, or high.

Underwriting Factors

☐ Low	☐ Moderate	☐ High

- Changes in underwriting standards including credit score, leverage, policies, price, tenor, collateral, guarantor support, covenants, and structure.
- The borrower's ability to service debt based on debt service coverage, debt/income ratios, and credit history.
- The volume and extent of exceptions and overrides.

Strategic Factors

☐ Low	☐ Moderate	☐ High

- The effect of strategic factors including the target market, the portfolio and product mix, acquisitions, diversification of repayment sources, new products and delivery channels, third-party originations, syndications, concentrations, and securitizations.
- The maintenance of an appropriate balance between risk and reward.

External Factors

☐ Low	☐ Moderate	☐ High

- The effect of external factors including, but not limited to, economic, industry, competitive, and market conditions; legislative and regulatory changes; and technological advancement.

Credit Quality Factors

☐ Low	☐ Moderate	☐ High

- The levels and trends of delinquencies, nonperforming and problem assets, losses, weighted average risk ratings, and reserves in both balance sheet and off-balance-sheet accounts.
- Trends in the growth and volume of lending and fee-based credit activities, including off-balance-sheet, syndication, investment, payment, settlement, and clearing activities.
- Trends in the financial performance of borrowers and counterparties.

- Trends identified in loan pricing methods, portfolio analytics and models, loss forecasting, and stress testing methods.
- Trends in summary ratings assigned by the bank's loan review and audit.
- Effect of credit enhancement on underwriting standards and level of risk.

Quality of Credit Risk Management

Examiners consider the following assessment factors when making judgments about the quality of credit risk management. These factors are the minimum **standards** that all examiners consider during every supervisory cycle to ensure quality supervision. Examiners should apply the standards consistent with the guidelines in the "Loan Portfolio Management" booklet of the *Comptroller's Handbook*. Examiners are required to judge, based on the review of the core assessment factors, whether risk management is strong, satisfactory, or weak.

Policies

☐ Strong	☐ Satisfactory	☐ Weak

- The consistency of the credit policy with the bank's overall strategic direction and risk tolerance or limits.
- The appropriate balance within the credit culture between credit and marketing.
- The structure of the credit operation and whether responsibility and accountability are assigned at every level.
- The reasonableness of definitions that guide policy, underwriting, and documentation exceptions and of guidelines for approving policy exceptions.
- The appropriateness of credit policies that establish risk limits or positions, including concentration limits, whether the bank requires periodic revaluation, and whether policies delineate prudent actions to be taken if the limits are broken.
- The approval of the credit policy by the board or an appropriate committee of the board.
- Consistency of underwriting expectations whether facilities are originated to hold or to distribute.

Processes

☐ Strong	☐ Satisfactory	☐ Weak

- The adequacy of processes that communicate policies and expectations to appropriate personnel.
- The production of timely, accurate, complete and relevant management information, including the aggregation of exposures across business lines.
- The adequacy of processes and systems to ensure compliance with policy.
- The appropriateness of the approval, monitoring, and reporting process for policy exceptions.
- The adequacy of internal control, including segregation of duties, dual control, authority commensurate with duties, etc.

- The capabilities of the front- and back-office systems to support current and projected credit operations.
- The adequacy of processes in place to address risk exposures associated with off-balance-sheet entities.
- The use and management of capital market products to manage risk.

Credit Granting
- The appropriateness of the approval process, marketing campaigns, and delivery channels.
- The adequacy of risk management processes related to syndicated loan pipeline management.
- The thoroughness of the underwriting analysis, including a sensitivity analysis of borrower projections.
- The sufficiency and reliability of methods used to analyze the creditworthiness of counterparties and debt issuers to ensure repayment capacity.
- The quality of analytical resources, such as scoring systems and portfolio models, and the adequacy of their periodic revalidation.

Credit Monitoring
- The adequacy of portfolio management, including the ability to identify, measure, and monitor risk relating to credit structure and avoiding undue concentrations.
- The adequacy of portfolio stress testing, rescoring, and behavioral scoring practices.
- The adequacy of credit analysis, including financial assessment and comparison of projections to actual performance.
- The frequency and reliability of verifying compliance with covenants.
- The accuracy and integrity of internal risk rating processes.

Collection Efforts
- The development and execution of action plans and collection strategies to facilitate timely collection.
- The timely involvement of a specialized collection unit.

ALLL & Accounting Controls
- The method of evaluating and maintaining the allowance for loan and lease losses.
- Compliance with regulatory and accounting standards and guidelines.

Personnel

☐ Strong	☐ Satisfactory	☐ Weak

- The depth of technical and managerial expertise.
- The appropriateness of performance management and compensation programs. Such programs should exclude incentives for personnel to take excessive risks.
- The appropriateness of management's response to deficiencies identified in policies, processes, personnel, and control systems.
- The level of turnover of critical staff.

- The adequacy of training.
- The ability of managers to implement new products, services, and systems in response to changing business, economic, or competitive conditions.
- The understanding of and adherence to the bank's strategic direction and risk tolerance as defined by senior management and the board.

Control Systems

☐ Strong	☐ Satisfactory	☐ Weak

- The timeliness, accuracy, completeness, and relevance of management information systems, reports, monitoring, and control functions.
- The scope, frequency, and independence of the risk review, quality assurance, and internal/external audit functions.
- The effectiveness of quality assurance and audit functions in identifying deficiencies in policy, processes, personnel, and internal control.
- The independent use and validation of measurement controls.
- The effectiveness of exception monitoring systems that identify, measure, and track incremental risk exposure by how much (in frequency and amount) the exceptions deviate from policy and established limits, and the adequacy of corrective actions.
- The appropriateness of model validation activities.
- The adequacy, independence, and consistent application of valuation methodologies supporting the fair value estimates of complex and other illiquid instruments.
- The effectiveness of risk rating systems, quantification methods, and data maintenance systems utilized in the bank's efforts to report under the Basel II Advanced Internal Ratings-Based (A-IRB) approach.

Interest Rate Risk

Quantity of Interest Rate Risk

Examiners consider the following assessment factors when making judgments about the quantity of interest rate risk. These factors are the minimum **standards** that all examiners consider during every supervisory cycle to ensure quality supervision. Examiners are required to judge, based on the review of the core assessment factors, whether the risk is low, moderate, or high.

Repricing Risk

☐ Low	☐ Moderate	☐ High

- The repricing mismatch of assets and liabilities over the short-term and long-term.
- The adequacy of repricing distribution assumptions for nonmaturity deposit balances.
- The volume of non-interest income streams that may be interest rate sensitive.
- The vulnerability of earnings and capital to large interest rate changes, such as rate shocks and gradual rate shifts, e.g., a change of 200 basis points over 12 months.
- The presence of over-the-counter and exchange-traded derivatives, such as futures and interest rate swaps, used for rebalancing repricing mismatches.

Basis Risk

☐ Low	☐ Moderate	☐ High

- The use of different indexes to price assets and liabilities (e.g., prime, Constant Maturity Treasury, Libor, and 11th District Cost of Funds Index) that may change at different times or by different amounts.
- Lagged or asymmetric pricing behavior in bank-managed rates such as the rates on consumer deposits.
- The effect of changes in cash flow and repricing *correlations* between hedging instruments and the positions being hedged.

Yield Curve Risk

☐ Low	☐ Moderate	☐ High

- The exposure of on- and off-balance-sheet positions to changes in the yield curve's absolute level and shape (e.g., rising level with flattening slope, falling level with steepening slope, curve inverts, and twists).

Options Risk

☐ Low	☐ Moderate	☐ High

- The extent of written (sold) options embedded in assets (e.g., loan and mortgage prepayments, interest rate caps and floors embedded in adjustable rate loans, and callable securities).
- The potential effect of written options embedded in liabilities (e.g., early deposit withdrawals, nonmaturity deposit elasticities, and callable liabilities).
- The volume of over-the-counter and exchange-traded options contracts.

Strategic Factors

☐ Low	☐ Moderate	☐ High

- The ability of the funding strategy to tolerate adverse interest rate movements.
- The effect of the bank's overall business strategy on interest rate risk (e.g., entering into new business activities, speculating on the direction and volatility of interest rates, investing in supporting technology).

External Factors

☐ Low	☐ Moderate	☐ High

- The ability to withstand changes in interest rates caused by external factors including, but not limited to, economic conditions, industry conditions, legislative and regulatory changes, market demographics, technological changes, competition, and market conditions.

Quality of Interest Rate Risk Management

Examiners consider the following assessment factors when making judgments about the quality of interest rate risk management. These factors are the minimum **standards** that all examiners consider during every supervisory cycle to ensure quality supervision. Examiners are required to judge, based on the review of the core assessment factors, whether risk management is strong, satisfactory, or weak.

Policies

☐ Strong	☐ Satisfactory	☐ Weak

- The consistency of the interest rate risk policy with the bank's overall strategic direction and risk tolerance or limits.
- The structure of the interest rate risk management function and whether responsibility and accountability are assigned at every level.
- The appropriateness of guidelines that establish risk limits or positions, including requirements that the guidelines be periodically reassessed, and whether the guidelines delineate prudent actions to be taken if the limits are broken.
- The reasonableness of definitions that guide policy exceptions and guidelines for approving policy exceptions.

- The approval of the interest rate risk policy by the board or an appropriate committee of the board.
- The existence of adequate standards, given the bank's price risk, for validating an independent model.

Processes

□ Strong	□ Satisfactory	□ Weak

- The adequacy of processes that communicate policies and expectations to appropriate personnel.
- The production of timely, accurate, complete, and relevant management information.
- The adequacy of processes and systems to ensure compliance with policy.
- The appropriateness of the approval, monitoring, and reporting process for policy exceptions.
- The adequacy of risk measurement systems to capture material positions, both on- and off-balance-sheet, and the risks inherent in the positions.
- The extent of clearly defined and reasonable measurement assumptions.
- The adequacy of internal control, including segregation of duties, dual control, authority commensurate with duties, etc.
- The sufficiency of periodic stress tests that use scenarios reducing or eliminating profits and the tests' capacity to project accurately the effect of certain conditions.
- An understanding of the vulnerability to limitations or weaknesses of measurement tools.
- The adequacy of the risk measurement process to consider both risk to earnings and risk to capital.
- The extent of consideration given to the effect of changing rates on noninterest income and expenses.
- The flexibility to modify positions in adverse rate environments in a timely manner.
- The reasonableness of responses to changes in market conditions.
- The capabilities of the front- and back-office systems to support current and projected interest rate processes.

Personnel

□ Strong	□ Satisfactory	□ Weak

- The depth of technical and managerial expertise.
- The appropriateness of performance management and compensation programs. Such programs should exclude incentives for personnel to take excessive risks.
- The appropriateness of management's response to deficiencies identified in policies, processes, personnel, and control systems.
- The level of turnover of critical staff.
- The adequacy of training.
- The ability of managers to implement new products, services, and systems in response to changing business, economic, and competitive conditions.
- The ability of risk management to identify and manage the risks involved in new products, services, and systems, especially those of a complex nature.

- The understanding of and adherence to the bank's strategic direction and risk tolerance as defined by senior management and the board.

Control Systems

☐ Strong	☐ Satisfactory	☐ Weak

- The timeliness, accuracy, completeness, and relevance of management information systems, reports, monitoring, and control functions.
- The scope, frequency, effectiveness, and independence of the risk review, quality assurance, and internal/external audit functions.
- The effectiveness of control systems to identify and prevent internal control deficiencies.
- The existence of an independent and competent audit function that validates the reliability and effectiveness of models and management processes.
- The independence of risk-monitoring and control functions from the risk- taking function(s).
- The independence and validation of models and other measurement tools and the validity of assumptions.

Liquidity Risk

Quantity of Liquidity Risk

Examiners consider the following assessment factors when making judgments about the quantity of liquidity risk. These factors are the minimum **standards** that all examiners consider during every supervisory cycle to ensure quality supervision. Examiners are required to judge, based on the review of the core assessment factors, whether the risk is low, moderate, or high.

Wholesale Liabilities

☐ Low	☐ Moderate	☐ High

- The volume, composition, growth trends, and projections.
- The level of credit sensitivity.
- The level of customer loyalty generated through direct relationship management.
- The tenor, rates paid, and collateralization requirements of FHLB advances, repurchase agreements, and uninsured deposit products (e.g., CDs, MMDAs, other savings, and brokered deposits).

Retail Liabilities

☐ Low	☐ Moderate	☐ High

- The volume, composition, growth trends, and projections.
- The deposit mix.
- The loyalty and stability of the customer base.
- The tenor and rates paid on insured deposit products (e.g., CDs, MMDAs, savings, brokered deposits, etc.).

Diversification

☐ Low	☐ Moderate	☐ High

- The extent to which liabilities are diversified by individual funds provider, product, tenor, market area, industry, etc.
- The sufficiency of diversity by marketer (i.e., individual broker or through direct placement).
- The appropriateness of investment objectives or economic influences.
- The extent of asset diversification as evidenced by the variety of loans and investments or other assets that the bank could use to raise funds.

On- and Off-balance-sheet Cash Flows

☐ Low	☐ Moderate	☐ High

- The capacity to access additional unsecured market funding

- In the current environment.
- In a distressed environment.
- The existence of current and projected securitization activities and associated cash flows, either as a source or potential use of funds including
  - The extent of reliance on cash flows from securitization activities (i.e., is securitization used occasionally to enhance liquidity or is it "pipeline" financing required for ongoing business?).
  - The existence of concentrations by maturity dates, products, purchasers, or counterparties.
  - Compliance with covenants.
  - The depth and breadth of secondary markets.
  - The potential for early amortization (use of funds).
- The presence of other off-balance-sheet items which could result in cash flows to or from the balance sheet including
  - Unused loan commitments.
  - Letters of credit or other contingent liabilities.
  - Collateral requirement agreements.
  - Early liability termination arrangements.
  - Calls, options.
  - The inability to complete planned securitization activities or asset sales.

Net Funding Gaps

☐ Low	☐ Moderate	☐ High

- The volume of on- and off-balance-sheet net funding gaps.
- The extent of short- and long-term cash flow gaps in the existing structure.
- The projected growth or depletion of assets and liabilities.
- The extent of dependence on credit-sensitive sources.
- The adequacy of current and projected cash flow projections in normal environments (i.e., day-to-day activities), as well as in significantly deteriorated environments (usually best demonstrated in the contingency funding plan).
- The ability to cover projected funding gaps when needed in a cost-effective manner.

External and Environmental Factors

☐ Low	☐ Moderate	☐ High

- How external sources of liquidity view the bank's current and projected
  - Asset quality, earnings, and capital.
  - Reputation risk or other credit-sensitive factors that could influence customer behavior.
- The effect of the parent company's and affiliate's current and projected
  - Asset quality, earnings, and capital.
  - Liquidity, especially relating to commercial paper coverage.
  - Reputation risk, strategic risk, or other factors that could influence customer behavior.
- The effect of the external market environment including

- Bank rating agency ratings and trends.
- Relative cost of funds (credit default swap or debt spreads over comparable U.S. Treasury securities, compared with those of competitors).
- Economic conditions, including job growth, migration, industry concentrations, competition, etc.
- The depth and breadth of the market.
- System-wide shocks to markets and market participants.

Liquid Asset-based Factors

☐ Low	☐ Moderate	☐ High

- The relationship of volume and trends in liquid assets compared with volume and trends of liabilities.
- The volume and composition of money market assets such as fed funds sold, Eurodollars placed, and certificates of deposit (CDs) purchased.
- The volume, composition, and trend of unencumbered highly liquid assets the bank can sell or pledge under both business as usual and distressed conditions. Consider
    - The level of unencumbered highly liquid assets compared to liquidity needs as well as the duration and severity of the liquidity stress.
    - Intraday liquidity needs.
    - Asset valuation under distressed conditions.
    - Central bank collateral requirements.
- The amount of depreciation in the investment portfolio.
- The appropriateness of the unit size of investment securities to provide for effective use.
- The capacity to enhance liquidity through asset sales or securitization.
- The bank's experience in asset sales or securitization markets.

Quality of Liquidity Risk Management

Examiners consider the following assessment factors when making judgments about the quality of liquidity risk management. These factors are the minimum **standards** that all examiners consider during every supervisory cycle to ensure quality supervision. Examiners are required to judge, based on the review of the core assessment factors, whether risk management is strong, satisfactory, or weak.

Policies

☐ Strong	☐ Satisfactory	☐ Weak

- The consistency of the liquidity policy with the bank's overall business strategy, role in the financial system, and risk tolerance or limits.
- The appropriateness of stated limits.
- The appropriateness of guidelines for intraday liquidity, collateral management, diversification, and concentrations.
- Whether the policy establishes appropriate responsibilities and accountability at every level.

- The reasonableness of definitions that guide policy exceptions and guidelines for approving policy exceptions.
- The appropriateness of liquidity guidelines that establish risk limits or positions and whether periodic revaluation is required, and whether the guidelines delineate prudent actions to be taken if the limits or positions are broken.
- Whether the contingency funding plan (CFP) clearly establishes strategies that address liquidity shortfalls in a distressed environment.
- The appropriateness of stress testing requirements (i.e., includes both institution-specific and market-wide scenarios).
- The periodic approval of the liquidity policy by the board or an appropriate committee of the board.

Processes

☐ Strong	☐ Satisfactory	☐ Weak

- The adequacy of the financial planning and management strategy.
- The adequacy of processes communicating policies and expectations to appropriate personnel (starting with the asset-liability committee (ALCO) or similar committee).
- The adequacy of MIS reports that are timely, accurate, complete, and relevant (including the aggregation of exposures across business lines) in both a business as usual and a distressed environment.
- The adequacy of collateral management processes, including major asset class, monitoring by legal entity, and the ability of the custody or settlement system to operate within operational or timing requirements needed to deliver collateral when or where needed.
- The adequacy of processes to monitor on- and off-balance sheet cash flows, including access to additional funding, securitization activities, contingent liabilities, and collateral requirements.
- The adequacy of stress testing and whether stress test results cause changes in liquidity risk management strategies, policies, risk limits, and contingency funding plans. Consider
  - Illiquid assets markets.
  - Deposit run-off.
  - Availability of both secured and unsecured funding sources.
  - Margin calls and collateral requirements.
  - Funding tenors.
  - Potential draws on liquidity from off-balance-sheet or contingent claims.
  - Availability of contingent lines of credit.
  - Effect of asset quality deterioration or credit rating downgrades.
  - Ability to move funds across borders, currencies, and legal entities.
  - Access to central bank lending facilities.
  - Estimate of balance sheet changes.
- The appropriateness of the bank's CFP given the bank's complexity, risk profile, and its role within the financial system. Consider whether the CFP
  - Is integrated into the bank's overall liquidity risk management framework.

- Is adjusted to reflect the results of stress testing and covers a range of scenarios, including bank-specific and market-wide events.
- Clearly details a range of options available to management to meet potential liquidity shortfalls.
- Clearly specifies management's roles and responsibilities, including the authority to invoke the CFP.
- Includes clear communications with interested parties (e.g., employees, market participants, regulators, shareholders, etc.).
- Addresses intraday liquidity needs.
- Addresses testing processes.
- The adequacy of processes and systems to ensure compliance with policy.
- The appropriateness of the approval, monitoring, and reporting process for policy exceptions.
- The adequacy of internal control, including segregation of duties, dual control, authority commensurate with duties, etc.
- The capabilities of the front- and back-office systems to support current and projected operations.

Personnel

☐ Strong	☐ Satisfactory	☐ Weak

- The depth of technical and managerial expertise.
- The appropriateness of the performance management and compensation programs. Such programs should exclude incentives for personnel to take excessive risks.
- The appropriateness of management's response to deficiencies identified in policies, processes, personnel, and control systems.
- The level of turnover of critical staff.
- The adequacy of training.
- The ability of managers to implement new products, services, and systems in response to changing business, economic, competitive conditions.
- The understanding of and adherence to the bank's strategic direction and risk tolerance as defined by senior management and the board.

Control Systems

☐ Strong	☐ Satisfactory	☐ Weak

- The timeliness, accuracy, completeness, and relevance of management information systems, reports, monitoring, and control functions.
- The scope, frequency, effectiveness, and independence of the risk review, quality assurance, and internal/external audit functions.
- The effectiveness of control systems to identify and prevent internal control deficiencies.
- The appropriateness of limits governing balance sheet composition (ratios), cash flow (funding gaps), and diversification (concentrations), as well as the appropriateness of limits on the amount provided by any one source of funds.

- The existence of an independent and competent audit function that validates the reliability and effectiveness of models and management processes.
- The independence of risk-monitoring and control functions from the risk- taking function(s).
- The independence and validation of models and other measurement tools, and the validity of assumptions.

Price Risk

Quantity of Price Risk

Examiners consider the following assessment factors when making judgments about the quantity of price risk. These factors are the minimum **standards** that all examiners consider during every supervisory cycle to ensure quality supervision. Examiners are required to judge, based on the review of the core assessment factors, whether the risk is low, moderate, or high.

Volume of Open Positions

☐ Low	☐ Moderate	☐ High

- The level of open positions expressed as earnings and/or capital at risk.
- The level of open positions as compared to historical trading revenues, risk limits, and economic capital.
- The size of illiquid positions.
- The total volume of assets and liabilities accounted for at fair value through earnings.
- The size of held-for-sale loan portfolios.
- The level of capital subject to revaluation from currency translation requirements.

Market Factors

☐ Low	☐ Moderate	☐ High

- The price sensitivity to various market factors (e.g., foreign exchange, interest rates, equity, or commodity prices) in portfolios without options (linear portfolios).
- The sensitivity of mortgage servicing rights to valuation inputs (interest rates, prepayments, and volatilities).

Options Risk

☐ Low	☐ Moderate	☐ High

- The existence of nonlinear price sensitivity to changes in market factors.
- The existence of discontinuous option exposure (e.g., the exposure arising from path-dependent options).
- The level of options employed to hedge mortgage servicing rights.

Basis Risk

☐ Low	☐ Moderate	☐ High

- The volume of potential exposure caused by a change in the correlation between two prices (e.g., when the price of a derivative instrument and the price of its hedged asset do not move in tandem).

- The volume of potential exposure between the underlying mortgage rate and hedging instruments (TBAs, swaps, swaptions) for mortgage servicing rights.

Concentration of Factors

☐ Low	☐ Moderate	☐ High

- The level and diversification among products or types of products.
- The existence of concentrations in market factors (e.g., option strike prices).
- The existence of a dominant position in products and markets.
- Large positions concentrated in higher risk counterparties.

Product Liquidity

☐ Low	☐ Moderate	☐ High

- The volume of readily marketable products that generally can be liquidated or hedged within a reasonable time frame.
- The volume of illiquid products whose prices may decline because managers need a relatively long time to liquidate or effectively hedge them.
- The volume of Level 3 exposures (i.e., assets or liabilities with fair value measurement inputs that may not be readily observable in the market).
- The trend and volume of margin call disputes with counterparties.

Stability of Revenue

☐ Low	☐ Moderate	☐ High

- Revenue derived from customer-initiated trades in proportion to revenue derived from proprietary trading activity.
- Revenue derived from portfolio management activity.
- Revenue derived from changes in credit spreads.
- Mismatches in mortgage servicing rights and hedging revenues.

Quality of Price Risk Management

Examiners consider the following assessment factors when making judgments about the quality of price risk management. These factors are the minimum **standards** that all examiners consider during every supervisory cycle to ensure quality supervision. Examiners are required to judge, based on the review of the core assessment factors, whether risk management is strong, satisfactory, or weak.

Policies

☐ Strong	☐ Satisfactory	☐ Weak

- The consistency of policies related to activities creating price risk with the bank's overall strategic direction and risk tolerance or limits.

- The structure of the risk-taking operation and whether responsibility and accountability are assigned at every level.
- The reasonableness of the definitions that guide policy exceptions, the guidelines for approving policy exceptions, and the reporting requirements for those exceptions.
- The appropriateness of price risk guidelines that establish limits or positions, whether periodic revaluation is required, and whether the guidelines delineate prudent actions to be taken if the limits or positions are broken.
- The approval of policies by the board or an appropriate committee of the board.
- The existence of adequate standards for independent model validation given the bank's price risk.
- The appropriateness of polices that establish goals for and set limits on mortgage servicing rights, lending pipelines, and held-for-sale loan portfolios.
- The appropriateness of polices to address foreign currency translation hedging requirements and standards.

Processes

☐ Strong	☐ Satisfactory	☐ Weak

- The adequacy of risk measurement systems to capture material positions and the risks inherent in the positions.
- The adequacy of processes that communicate policies and expectations to appropriate personnel.
- The production of timely, accurate, complete, and relevant management information.
- The comprehensiveness of the strategic planning process.
- The adequacy of process controls over new product and systems development.
- The adequacy of processes and systems to ensure compliance with policy.
- The appropriateness of trading management oversight (i.e., approving and monitoring compliance with limits, communicating policies and expectations to appropriate personnel).
- The adequacy of independent measurement and analysis of risk under a variety of scenarios, including stress tests.
- The adequacy of the models used for testing revenue vulnerability under probable and stress test scenarios.
- The adequacy of processes used to identify and evaluate low-probability, high-impact exposures.
- The effectiveness of the profit and loss "explain" function (i.e., the process through which management breaks down trading results into their various components).
- The independence and adequacy of valuation processes and the validity of assumptions.
- The frequency of back-test exceptions.
- The appropriateness of the approval, monitoring, and reporting process for policy exceptions.
- The adequacy of internal control for trading operations (front- and back-office) including segregation of duties, dual control, authority commensurate with duties, etc.
- The capabilities of the front-, middle-, and back-office systems to support current and projected trading operations.

- The ability to aggregate price risk across trading desks and business lines.
- The adequacy of risk modeling for mortgage servicing rights including whether it is timely, complete, product specific (e.g., a sub-prime model is used for sub-prime loans), and reflects current market practices.

Personnel

☐ Strong	☐ Satisfactory	☐ Weak

- The depth of technical and managerial expertise.
- The appropriateness of performance management and compensation programs. Such programs should exclude incentives for personnel to take excessive risks.
- The appropriateness of management's response to deficiencies identified in policies, processes, personnel, and control systems.
- The level of turnover of critical staff.
- The adequacy of training.
- The ability of managers to implement new products, services, and systems in response to changing business, economic, or competitive conditions.
- The understanding of and adherence to the bank's strategic direction and risk tolerance as defined by senior management and the board.

Control Systems

☐ Strong	☐ Satisfactory	☐ Weak

- The timeliness, accuracy, completeness, and relevance of management information systems, reports, monitoring, and control functions.
- The adequacy and independence of validation processes for trading models and methods.
- The frequency and reliability of revaluations of individual position-taking.
- The potential exposure to trading losses as measured under normal and adverse scenarios.
- The scope, frequency, effectiveness, and independence of the risk review, quality assurance, and internal/external audit functions.
- The responsiveness of control systems to prevent and respond to internal control deficiencies.
- The independence of risk-monitoring and control functions from the risk- taking function(s).

Operational Risk

Quantity of Operational Risk

Examiners consider the following assessment factors when making judgments about the quantity of operational risk. These factors are the minimum **standards** that all examiners consider during every supervisory cycle to ensure quality supervision. Examiners are required to judge, based on the review of the core assessment factors, whether the risk is low, moderate, or high.

Structural Factors

☐ Low	☐ Moderate	☐ High

- The volume, type, and complexity of transactions, products, and services offered through the bank.
- The volume and severity of operational, administrative, personnel, and accounting control errors.
- The level and trend of operational loss events resulting from inadequate or failed internal processes or systems, the misconduct or errors of people, and adverse external events.
- The condition, security, capacity, and recoverability of systems.
- The complexity and volume of conversions, integrations, and system changes.
- The volume and type of activities and operations that have been outsourced or moved offshore.

Strategic Factors

☐ Low	☐ Moderate	☐ High

- The effect of strategy, including the development of new markets, products, services, technology, and delivery systems to maintain or enhance competitive position.
- The effect of acquisition and divestiture strategies on a market, product, and geographic basis.
- The approach towards hedging of operational risk and the extent to which management has evaluated its overall exposure and taken specific hedging actions, including insurance (e.g., self insurance or third-party purchase).
- The maintenance of an appropriate balance between technology innovation and secure operations.

External Factors

☐ Low	☐ Moderate	☐ High

- The effect of external factors including economic, industry, competitive, and market conditions; legislative and regulatory changes; and technological advancement.
- The effect of accounting changes (U.S. and abroad) on the institution and its operations.

- The effect of infrastructure threats on the bank's ability to deliver timely support and service.
- The ability of service providers to provide and maintain performance that meets the requirements of the bank.

Quality of Operational Risk Management

Examiners consider the following assessment factors when making judgments about the quality of operational risk management. These factors are the minimum **standards** that all examiners consider during every supervisory cycle to ensure quality supervision. Examiners are required to judge, based on the review of the core assessment factors, whether risk management is strong, satisfactory, or weak.

Policies

☐ Strong	☐ Satisfactory	☐ Weak

- The scope and coverage of the policies, given the institution's operations (lines of business and functional areas), risk profile, and strategic direction.
- The consistency of policy implementation across the organization.
- The adequacy of the governance structure around operational risk and the assignment of responsibility and accountability at every level.
- The reasonableness of definitions that guide policy exceptions and guidelines for approving policy exceptions.
- The periodic review and approval of policies by the board or an appropriate committee of the board.
- The appropriateness of guidelines that establish risk limits or tolerances, whether there is a periodic revaluation of those limits, and whether there is consideration given to actions to be taken if the limits are broken.
- The existence and adequacy of any standards for validating models.

Processes

☐ Strong	☐ Satisfactory	☐ Weak

- The integration of an effective operational risk management function into the corporation and each line-of-business.
- The adequacy of processes that communicate policies and expectations to appropriate personnel.
- The adequacy of processes that ensure that line of business policies are consistent with umbrella policies developed at the corporate level.
- The adequacy of processes and systems to ensure compliance with policy.
- The appropriateness of the approval, monitoring, and reporting process for policy exceptions.
- The adequacy of internal control, including segregation of duties, dual control, authority commensurate with duties, etc.

- The incorporation of project management into daily operations (e.g., systems development, capacity planning, change control, due diligence, and outsourcing).
- The adequacy of processes defining the systems architecture for transaction processing and for delivering products and services.
- The effectiveness of processes to ensure the integrity and security of systems.
- The adequacy of documentation supporting the operational risk framework.
- The adequacy of processes to ensure the reliability and retention of information (i.e., data creation, processing, storage, and delivery).
- The adequacy of processes to capture and track operational loss events, including clear definitions of what is to be captured and well-supported thresholds for capture.
- The adequacy of processes within the organization to ensure the proper functioning of controls.
- The adequacy of processes to detect and prevent internal and external fraud.
- The quality of physical and logical security to protect the confidentiality of consumer and corporate information.
- The capabilities of the front- and back-office systems to support current and projected operations.
- The adequacy of corporate contingency planning and business resumption covering both technology and physical infrastructure across the organization.
- The adequacy of the new product process, including consideration of BSA/AML/OFAC, consumer protection, and other laws and regulations. (Updated 9/28/2012)
- The adequacy of contracts and the ability to monitor relationships with vendors and third-party service providers.
- The ability to monitor activities and operations that have been moved offshore.
- The development of information technology solutions that meet the needs of end users.
- The capacity to deliver timely services and to respond rapidly to normal service interruptions or to attacks and intrusions from external sources.
- The appropriateness of risk measurement systems for the nature and complexity of activities, and how these systems are incorporated into the decision-making process.
- The effectiveness of management response to audit findings on control environment concerns.

Personnel

☐ Strong	☐ Satisfactory	☐ Weak

- The capability of the corporate operational risk management function in implementing tools to identify, measure, and monitor operational risk across the organization.
- The depth of technical and managerial expertise in both the operational risk management functions and throughout the organization in ensuring that risks are managed and controls are working as designed.
- The appropriateness of performance management and compensation programs, including accountability for compliance with BSA/AML/OFAC, consumer protection, and other laws and regulations. Such programs should exclude incentives for personnel to take excessive risks. (Updated 9/28/2012)

- The role of operational risk management and the extent to which it is independent of the lines of business.
- The ability of the internal audit staff to identify risk and control breakdowns and ensure appropriate remediation.
- The appropriateness of management's response to identified deficiencies in policies, processes, personnel, and control systems.
- The independence of operating staff.
- The level of turnover of critical staff.
- The adequacy of training at the corporate level, within the lines of business, and in the functional areas.
- Management's responsiveness to regulatory, accounting, industry, and technological changes.
- The ability of managers to implement new products, services, and systems in response to changing business, economic, or competitive conditions, while considering the risk these new ventures pose to the organization.
- The understanding of and adherence to the strategic direction and risk tolerance as defined by senior management and the board.
- The appropriateness of management hiring practices as a mechanism to deter internal fraud (e.g., background checks).

Control Systems

☐ Strong	☐ Satisfactory	☐ Weak

- The timeliness, accuracy, completeness, and relevance of management information systems, reports, monitoring (including transaction and surveillance monitoring systems used to detect and report suspicious activity), and control functions. (Updated 9/28/2012)
- The production of timely, accurate, complete, and relevant operational risk management and measurement reports to line of business managers, senior management, and the board of directors.
- The quality of the control environment and the extent to which controls are relevant given the institution's operations, risk profile, and overall trends in operational risk events in the institution.
- The comprehensiveness of the internal risk and control self-assessment structure or the development of such a structure.
- The scope, frequency, effectiveness, and independence of the risk review, quality assurance, and internal/external audit functions.
- The effectiveness of exception monitoring systems that identify, measure, and track incremental risk exposure by how much (in frequency and amount) the exceptions deviate from policy and established limits, and the adequacy of corrective actions.
- The independent testing of processes, including key controls, to ensure ongoing reliability and integrity of the risk management framework.
- The adequacy of systems to monitor capacity and performance.
- The adequacy of controls over new product and systems development.
- The adequacy of controls over activities and operations that have been outsourced or moved offshore.

Compliance Risk

Quantity of Compliance Risk

Examiners consider the following assessment factors when making judgments about the quantity of compliance risk. These factors are the minimum **standards** that all examiners consider during every supervisory cycle to ensure quality supervision. Examiners are required to judge, based on the review of the core assessment factors, whether the risk is low, moderate, or high.

Business Activity

☐ Low	☐ Moderate	☐ High

- The nature and extent of business activities, including rapid growth, new or unique products and services, delivery channels, third-party relationships, and significant merger and acquisition activity.
- The number of high-risk products, services, customers, and geographies for money laundering and terrorist financing activities. (Updated 9/28/2012)
- The level of competition and nature and extent of advertising and marketing activities.
- The span of the organization over supervisory and legal jurisdictions.

Litigation and Noncompliance

☐ Low	☐ Moderate	☐ High

- The amount and significance of litigation, monetary penalties, and customer complaints.
- The level of inquiries or investigations from other governmental agencies.
- The volume and significance of noncompliance and nonconformance with policies and procedures, laws, regulations, prescribed practices, and ethical standards.

Quality of Compliance Risk Management

Examiners consider the following assessment factors when making judgments about the quality of compliance risk management. These factors are the minimum **standards** that all examiners consider during every supervisory cycle to ensure quality supervision. Examiners are required to judge, based on the review of the core assessment factors, whether risk management is strong, satisfactory, or weak.

Policies

☐ Strong	☐ Satisfactory	☐ Weak

- The appropriateness of established policies and risk limits.
- The consistency of policies with the banks' overall strategic direction.
- The structure of the compliance risk management system and whether responsibility and accountability are assigned at every level.

- The reasonableness of definitions that determine policy exceptions and guidelines for approving policy exceptions.
- The periodic review of the effectiveness of the compliance risk management system, the BSA/AML and OFAC compliance programs, and approval of compliance policies by the board or an appropriate committee of the board. (Updated 9/28/2012)

Processes

□ Strong	□ Satisfactory	□ Weak

- The strength of the organization's compliance culture.
- The adequacy of processes communicating policies and expectations and changes to such policies and expectations to appropriate personnel.
- The adequacy of processes to capture and respond to consumer complaints and identify potential compliance issues.
- The adequacy of processes and systems to ensure compliance with policy and applicable laws and regulations, including BSA/AML/OFAC. (Updated 9/28/2012)
- The appropriateness of the approval, monitoring, and reporting process for policy exceptions.
- The adequacy of internal control, including segregation of duties, dual control, authority commensurate with duties, etc.
- The capabilities of the front- and back-office systems to support current and projected operations.
- The adequacy of processes assimilating legislative and regulatory changes into all aspects of the company.
- The adequacy of the budget to ensure that appropriate resources are allocated to compliance risk management and training.
- The extent to which violations, noncompliance, or weaknesses in the compliance risk management system are identified internally and corrected.
- The adequacy of integrating compliance considerations into all phases of corporate planning, including the development of new products and services.

Personnel

□ Strong	□ Satisfactory	□ Weak

- The depth of technical and managerial expertise.
- The appropriateness of performance management and compensation programs, including accountability for compliance with BSA/AML/OFAC, consumer protection, and other laws and regulations. Such programs should exclude incentives for personnel to take excessive risks. (Updated 9/28/2012)
- The appropriateness of management's response to deficiencies identified in policies, processes, personnel, and control systems.
- The independence of compliance staff. (Updated 9/28/2012)
- The level of turnover of critical staff.
- The adequacy of training.
- The adequacy of employee screening processes.

- The understanding of and adherence to the bank's strategic direction and risk tolerance as defined by senior management and the board.

Control Systems

☐ Strong	☐ Satisfactory	☐ Weak

- The timeliness, accuracy, completeness, and relevance of management information systems, reports, monitoring (including transaction and surveillance monitoring systems used to detect and report suspicious activity), and control functions. (Updated 9/28/2012)
- The scope, frequency, effectiveness, and independence of the risk review, quality assurance, and internal/external audit functions (including BSA/AML audits). (Updated 9/28/2012)
- The independent use and validation of measurement tools, systems, and programs, including those developed by third parties.
- The effectiveness of exception monitoring systems that identify, measure, and track incremental risk exposure by how much (in frequency and amount) the exceptions deviate from policy and established limits, and the adequacy of corrective actions.

Internal Control

Examiners consider the following assessment factors when making judgments about internal control. These factors are the minimum **standards** that all examiners consider during every supervisory cycle to ensure quality supervision. Examiners are required to judge, based on the review of the core assessment factors, whether internal control is strong, satisfactory, or weak.

Control Environment

☐ Strong	☐ Satisfactory	☐ Weak

- The integrity, ethical values, and competence of personnel.
- The organizational structure of the bank.
- Management's philosophy and operating style (i.e., strategic philosophy).
- External influences affecting operations and practices (e.g., independent audits, regulatory environment, and competitive and business markets).
- Methods of assigning authority and responsibility and of organizing and developing people.
- The attention and direction provided by the board of directors and its committees, especially the audit and risk management committees.

Risk Assessment

☐ Strong	☐ Satisfactory	☐ Weak

- Assessment of external and internal factors that could affect whether strategic objectives are achieved.
- Identification and analysis of risks.
- The systems used to manage and monitor the risks.
- Processes that react and respond to changing risk conditions.
- The competency, knowledge, and skills of personnel responsible for risk assessment.

Control Activities

☐ Strong	☐ Satisfactory	☐ Weak

- Policies and procedures established to ensure control processes are carried out.
- Reviews of operating activities.
- Approvals and authorization for transactions and activities.
- Segregation of duties.
- Vacation requirements or periodic rotation of duties for personnel in sensitive positions.
- Safeguarding access to, and use of, sensitive assets, records, and systems, including controls over material, non-public information.
- Independent checks or verifications of function performance and reconciliation of balances.
- Accountability.

Accounting, Information, and Communication

□ Strong	□ Satisfactory	□ Weak

- Management information systems that identify and capture relevant internal and external information in a timely manner.
- Accounting systems that ensure reporting of assets and liabilities in accordance with generally accepted accounting principles and regulatory requirements.
- Information systems that ensure effective communication of positions and activities.
- Contingency planning for information systems.

Self-assessment and Monitoring

□ Strong	□ Satisfactory	□ Weak

- Periodic evaluation of internal control whether by self-assessment or independent audit.[20]
- Systems to ensure timely and accurate reporting of deficiencies.
- Processes to ensure timely modification of policies and procedures, as needed.

---

[20] National banks may be subject to 12 CFR 363 and Section 404 of the Sarbanes-Oxley Act. For more information, refer to the "Internal and External Audits" booklet of the *Comptroller's Handbook.*

Audit

Examiners consider the following assessment factors when making judgments about audit. These factors are the minimum **standards** that all examiners consider during every supervisory cycle to ensure quality supervision. Examiners are required to judge, based on the review of the core assessment factors, whether audit is strong, satisfactory, or weak.

> **Note: Examiners should use expanded procedures,[21] including verification procedures, when significant control concerns are evident, in areas of greater complexity, and in areas with higher risk profiles. Internal audit may be a department of the bank or holding company, or an outsourced function.**

Audit Committee

☐ Strong	☐ Satisfactory	☐ Weak

- The composition and qualifications of the company's audit committee, and whether members are independent of management.
- The existence of an audit committee charter and the sufficiency of its content, dissemination, review, and approval.
- The audit committee's understanding of and compliance with its statutory duties and responsibilities pertaining to external audit's processes/ procedures, conclusions/findings, and reporting regarding the company's financial reporting control systems.
- The number of audit committee meetings held and the depth of those meetings.
- The engagement of discussions on new business ventures, the risks involved and planned controls.
- The effectiveness of reporting to the audit committee, including annual audit plans and performance against those plans, staffing and resources, quality assurance results, audit concerns, emerging issues, corrective actions, and exception tracking.
- The maintenance of an open dialogue with regulators and external auditors.
- The role of the committee in reviewing and approving audit plans and engagement letters.
- The role of the committee in overseeing the general auditor, including evaluating performance and setting compensation.

Audit Management & Processes

☐ Strong	☐ Satisfactory	☐ Weak

- The corporate culture and commitment to the audit function supporting an effective control environment.
- The independence of the audit function.

---

[21] Expanded procedures should be drawn from "Internal and External Audits" and other booklets of the *Comptroller's Handbook*. Internal control questionnaires and verification procedures can be found on *Examiner's Library* and the *e files* DVDs.

- The leadership and direction provided by audit management and their industry expertise and knowledge in relation to the sophistication and complexity of the bank's risk profile and operations.
- The effective and appropriate management of any outsourced or co-sourced audit activities or functions.
- The adequacy of audit plans, including the effectiveness of the audit planning horizon, the identification of the audit universe and auditable entities, and the integration of professional standards into the overall program.
- The flexibility of audit scopes regarding adding new business lines and merged activities.
- The timeliness, accuracy, and reliability of reports used to manage the audit unit.
- The accuracy of audit risk assessments and frequency of audits.
- The effectiveness of follow up actions, including whether they are timely and thorough.
- The effectiveness of audit involvement in mergers and acquisitions.

Audit Reporting

☐ Strong	☐ Satisfactory	☐ Weak

- The audit rating system's effectiveness and granularity.
- The timeliness of audit reports and whether they clearly outline the root causes of problems, specifically point out management issues when present, and identify areas of increased levels of control weaknesses.
- The effectiveness of the internal audit program's exception/correction-tracking system used to monitor and report significant control findings and open issues from all sources and to report on the status/adequacy of corrective actions to the audit committee.
- Work paper documentation on the adequacy of audit scope, coverage, and testing to assess the internal control environment in the audited unit, and to support the conclusions reached.[22]

Internal Audit Staff

☐ Strong	☐ Satisfactory	☐ Weak

- The independence of internal audit staff.
- The overall adequacy and competency of the internal audit staff, considering the level of risk undertaken by the bank, staff turnover, vacancies, recruitment, training, subject matter expertise, and professional certifications.
- The effectiveness of succession planning within the audit group.
- The level or reliance on outsourced internal audit activities.

---

[22] Guidance on work paper reviews is in the "Internal Control and Audit" section of the "Introduction."

Regulatory Ratings

Regulatory ratings must be assigned at least annually for each national bank in the company. Examiners consider the factors listed below when assigning regulatory ratings. These factors are the minimum **standards** that all examiners consider during every supervisory cycle to ensure quality supervision. Examiners are required to judge, based on the review of the core assessment, whether the composite and each component is rated 1, 2, 3, 4, or 5.[23]

> **Note:** While the regulatory ratings remain point-in-time judgments of a bank's financial, managerial, operational, and compliance performance, the description of each component contains explicit language emphasizing management's ability to manage risk. Therefore the conclusions drawn in the risk assessment system should be considered when assigning the corresponding component and the composite rating.

Capital Adequacy	1 ☐	2 ☐	3 ☐	4 ☐	5 ☐

- The level and quality of capital and the overall financial condition of the institution.
- The ability of management to address emerging needs for additional capital.
- The nature, trend, and volume of problem assets and the adequacy of allowances for loan and lease losses and other valuation reserves.
- Balance sheet composition, including the nature and amount of intangible assets, market risk, concentration risk, and risks associated with nontraditional activities.
- Risk exposure represented by off balance-sheet activities.
- The quality and strength of earnings, and the reasonableness of dividends.
- Prospects and plans for growth, as well as past experience in managing growth.
- Access to capital markets and other sources of capital, including support provided by a parent holding company.

Asset Quality	1 ☐	2 ☐	3 ☐	4 ☐	5 ☐

- The adequacy of underwriting standards, soundness of credit administration practices, and appropriateness of risk identification practices.
- The level, distribution, severity, and trend of problem, classified, nonaccrual, restructured, delinquent, and nonperforming assets for both on and off balance-sheet transactions.
- The adequacy of the allowance for loan and lease losses and other asset valuation reserves.
- The credit risk arising from or reduced by off balance-sheet transactions, such as unfunded commitments, credit derivatives, commercial and standby letters of credit, and lines of credit.

---

[23] The factors are extracted from the "Bank Supervision Process" booklet of the *Comptroller's Handbook* and reflect guidance in the Uniform Financial Institutions Rating System.

- The diversification and quality of the loan and investment portfolios.
- The extent of securities underwriting activities and exposure to counterparties in trading activities.
- The existence of asset concentrations.
- The adequacy of loan and investment policies, procedures, and practices.
- The ability of management to properly administer its assets, including the timely identification and collection of problem assets.
- The adequacy of internal control and management information systems.
- The volume and nature of credit documentation exceptions.

Management	1 ☐	2 ☐	3 ☐	4 ☐	5 ☐

- The level and quality of oversight and support of all institution activities by the board of directors and management.
- The ability of the board of directors and management, in their respective roles, to plan for and respond to risks that may arise from changing business conditions or the initiation of new activities or products.
- The adequacy of, and conformance with, appropriate internal policies and controls addressing the operations and risks of significant activities.
- The accuracy, timeliness, and effectiveness of management information and risk-monitoring systems appropriate for the institution's size, complexity, and risk profile.
- The adequacy of audits and internal control to promote effective operations and reliable financial and regulatory reporting; safeguard assets; and ensure compliance with laws, regulations, and internal policies.
- The adequacy of the compliance risk management process to ensure compliance with laws and regulations, including BSA/AML/OFAC. Note: Serious deficiencies in BSA/AML compliance create a presumption that the management component rating will be adversely affected because risk management practices are less than satisfactory. Support for incorporating BSA/AML examination findings into the management rating should be fully documented. (Updated 9/28/2012)
- Responsiveness to recommendations from auditors and supervisory authorities.
- Management depth and succession.
- The extent to which the board of directors and management is affected by, or susceptible to, a dominant influence or a concentration of authority.
- Reasonableness of compensation policies and avoidance of self dealing.
- Demonstrated willingness to serve the legitimate banking needs of the community.
- The overall performance of the institution and its risk profile.

Earnings	1 ☐	2 ☐	3 ☐	4 ☐	5 ☐

- The level of earnings, including trends and stability.
- The ability to provide for adequate capital through retained earnings.
- The quality and sources of earnings.

- The level of expenses in relation to operations.
- The adequacy of the budgeting systems, forecasting processes, and management information systems in general.
- The adequacy of provisions to maintain the allowance for loan and lease losses and other valuation allowance accounts.
- The earnings exposure to market risk such as interest rate, foreign currency translation, and price risks.

Liquidity	1 ☐	2 ☐	3 ☐	4 ☐	5 ☐

- The adequacy of liquidity sources compared with present and future needs and the ability of the institution to meet liquidity needs without adversely affecting its operations or condition.
- The availability of assets readily convertible to cash without undue loss.
- Access to money markets and other sources of funding.
- The level of diversification of funding sources, both on and off balance-sheet.
- The degree of reliance on short term, volatile sources of funds, including borrowings and brokered deposits, to fund longer term assets.
- The trend and stability of deposits.
- The ability to securitize and sell certain pools of assets.
- The capability of management to properly identify, measure, monitor, and control the institution's liquidity position, including the effectiveness of funds management strategies, liquidity policies, management information systems, and contingency funding plans.

Sensitivity to Market Risk	1 ☐	2 ☐	3 ☐	4 ☐	5 ☐

- The sensitivity of the financial institution's earnings or the economic value of its capital to adverse changes in interest rates, commodity prices, or equity prices.
- The ability of management to identify, measure, monitor, and control exposure to market risk given the institution's size, complexity, and risk profile.
- The nature and complexity of interest rate risk exposure arising from nontrading positions.
- If appropriate, the nature and complexity of market risk exposure arising from trading and foreign operations.

Information Technology	1 ☐	2 ☐	3 ☐	4 ☐	5 ☐

- The adequacy and effectiveness of the Information Technology risk management practices.

- Planning for and oversight of technological resources and services and ensuring that they support the bank's strategic goals and objectives, whether these services are obtained in-house or outsourced.
- The accuracy, reliability, and integrity of automated information and associated MIS, including the protection from unauthorized change.
- The protection of bank and customer information from accidental or inadvertent disclosure.
- The effectiveness and adequacy of business resumption and contingency planning.

Asset Management	1 ☐	2 ☐	3 ☐	4 ☐	5 ☐

- The level and quality of oversight and support of asset management activities by the board of directors and management, including committee structure and documentation of committee actions.
- The competence, experience, and knowledge of management with regard to the institution's business strategies, policies, procedures, and control systems.
- The adequacy of risk management practices and compliance programs relative to the size, complexity, and risk profile of the institution's asset management activities.
- The effectiveness and adequacy of policies and controls put in place to prevent and detect conflicts of interest, self-dealing, suspicious activity, and securities violations.
- The adequacy and consistency of policies and procedures given the institution's strategic plan, risk tolerances, and culture.
- The adequacy of staff, facilities, and operating systems; records, accounting, and data processing systems; segregation of duties; and trading functions and securities-lending activities.
- The level and consistency of profitability generated by the institution's asset management activities in relation to the volume and character of the institution's business.

Consumer Compliance	1 ☐	2 ☐	3 ☐	4 ☐	5 ☐

- The nature and extent of present compliance with consumer protection and civil rights statutes and regulations.
- The commitment of the board and management to compliance and their ability and willingness to ensure continuing compliance.
- The adequacy of operating systems, including internal procedures, controls, and audit activities, designed to ensure compliance on a routine and consistent basis.
- The degree of reliance that can be placed on the bank's risk management systems.

Composite Rating	1 ☐	2 ☐	3 ☐	4 ☐	5 ☐

In addition to the above factors, examiners should consider performance under Municipal and Government Securities Dealers requirements and the Community Reinvestment Act when assigning the composite rating. The CRA rating is assigned periodically through the issuance of a CRA performance evaluation.

Risk Assessment System

Conclusions from the core assessment allow examiners to assess the risk profile of the institution. Although the core assessment will normally only need to be completed in full annually, examiners complete a RAS summary for the *consolidated* company quarterly or more often if its risk profile or condition warrants it. One of these quarterly assessments accompanies the annual core assessment and includes a comprehensive narrative on the aggregate risk, direction of risk, and when applicable, quantity of risk and quality of risk management, for each risk category. The remaining quarterly assessments update the annual assessment and serve to highlight any changes in the company's or an individual bank's risk profile.

All RAS summaries should be documented in the OCC's supervisory information systems. Any appropriate changes to the supervisory strategy due to changes in the risk profile should also be documented in the OCC's supervisory information systems.

Strategic Risk

Strategic risk is the risk to current or anticipated earnings, capital, or franchise or enterprise value arising from adverse business decisions, poor implementation of business decisions, or lack of responsiveness to changes in the banking industry and operating environment. This risk is a function of a bank's strategic goals, business strategies, resources, and quality of implementation. The resources needed to carry out business strategies are both tangible and intangible. They include communication channels, operating systems, delivery networks, and managerial capacities and capabilities. (Updated 5/06/2013)

The assessment of strategic risk includes more than an analysis of a bank's written strategic plan. It focuses on opportunity costs and how plans, systems, and implementation affect the bank's franchise or enterprise value. It also incorporates how management analyzes external factors, such as economic, technological, competitive, regulatory, and other environmental changes, that affect the bank's strategic direction. (Updated 5/06/2013)

Summary Conclusions

Conclusions from the core assessment allow examiners to assess aggregate strategic risk and the direction of risk.

Aggregate strategic risk is:

☐ Low	☐ Moderate	☐ High

The direction of risk is expected to be:

☐ Decreasing	☐ Stable	☐ Increasing

Examiners use the following definitions to determine aggregate strategic risk. It is not necessary to meet every qualifier to be accorded a specific assessment.

- **Low** — Strategic decisions or external pressures are expected to nominally affect franchise or enterprise value. Exposure reflects strategic goals that are sound, highly compatible with the business direction, and responsive to changes in the environment. Initiatives are well-conceived and supported by capital, communication channels, operating systems, delivery networks, staff, and other resources. The depth and technical expertise of staff enables management to effectively set strategic direction and achieve organizational efficiency. Management has a successful record in accomplishing their stated strategic goals. Initiatives are supported by sound due diligence and effective risk management systems, which are an integral part of strategic planning. Strategic decisions can be reversed with only negligible cost or difficulty. Strategic goals and the corporate culture are effectively communicated and consistently applied throughout the organization. MIS effectively support strategic direction and initiatives. Management is aware of and effectively incorporates technology management into their strategic plans.

- **Moderate** — Strategic decisions or external pressures are not expected to significantly affect franchise or enterprise value. Exposure reflects strategic goals that, although aggressive, are compatible with the business direction and responsive to changes in the environment. Initiatives are usually well-conceived and supported by capital, communication channels, operating systems, delivery networks, staff, and other resources. Weaknesses in the depth and technical expertise of staff sometime prevent management from effectively setting strategic direction or achieving organizational efficiency. Management has a reasonable record accomplishing their stated strategic goals. Strategic decisions can be reversed without significant cost or difficulty. The quality of due diligence and risk management is consistent with the strategic issues confronting the organization. Risk management is not always an integral part of strategic planning. Strategic goals and the corporate culture are appropriately communicated and consistently applied throughout the organization. MIS reasonably support the company's strategic direction. Management is aware of and usually incorporates technology management into their strategic plans.

- **High** — Strategic decisions or external pressures are expected to adversely affect franchise or enterprise value. Strategic initiatives may be nonexistent, overly aggressive, incompatible with the business direction, or non-responsive to changes in the environment. Strategic decisions may be difficult or costly to reverse. Strategic goals may be nonexistent, poorly defined, or fail to consider changes in the business environment. Initiatives may be poorly conceived or inadequately supported by capital, communication channels, operating systems, delivery networks, staff, and other resources. Insufficient depth and technical expertise of staff often prevents management from effectively setting strategic direction and achieving organizational efficiency. Management does not consistently accomplish their stated strategic goal. Less than effective risk management systems or a lack of adequate due diligence has resulted in deficiencies in management decisions and may undermine effective evaluation of resources and commitment to new products and services, or acquisitions. Strategic goals and the corporate culture may not be clearly communicated and consistently applied throughout the organization. MIS may be insufficient to support the company's strategic direction or address a changing environment. Management ineffectively incorporates technology management into their strategic plans.

Reputation Risk

Reputation risk is the risk to current or anticipated earnings, capital, or franchise or enterprise value arising from negative public opinion. This risk may impair a bank's competitiveness by affecting its ability to establish new relationships or services or continue servicing existing relationships. Reputation risk is inherent in all bank activities and requires management to exercise an abundance of caution in dealing with customers, counterparties, correspondents, investors, and the community. (Updated 5/06/2013)

A bank that actively associates its name with products and services offered through outsourced arrangements or asset management affiliates is more likely to have higher reputation risk exposure. Significant threats to a bank's reputation also may result from negative publicity regarding matters such as unethical or deceptive business practices, violations of laws or regulations, high-profile litigation, or poor financial performance. The assessment of reputation risk should take into account the bank's culture, the effectiveness of its problem-escalation processes and rapid-response plans, and its deployment of media. (Updated 5/06/2013)

Summary Conclusions

Conclusions from the core assessment allow examiners to assess aggregate reputation risk and the direction of risk.

Aggregate reputation risk is:

☐ Low	☐ Moderate	☐ High

The direction of risk is expected to be:

☐ Decreasing	☐ Stable	☐ Increasing

Examiners use the following definitions to determine aggregate reputation risk. It is not necessary to meet every qualifier to be accorded a specific assessment.

- **Low** — The institution enjoys a favorable market and public perception. The level of litigation, losses, violations of laws and regulations, and customer complaints is minimal. The potential exposure to franchise or enterprise value is nominal relative to the number and type of accounts, the volume of assets under management, and the number of affected transactions. Management effectively self-polices risk and anticipates and responds well to changes of a market, technological or regulatory nature that affect its reputation in the marketplace. Management fosters a sound culture and administrative procedures and processes that are well-supported throughout the organization and have proven very successful over time. Management is well-versed in complex risks and has avoided conflicts of interest and other legal or control breaches. MIS, internal control, and audit are very effective. Management has a clear awareness of privacy issues and uses consumer information responsibly.

- **Moderate** — Vulnerability to changes in market and public perception is not material given the level of litigation, losses, violations of laws and regulations, and customer complaints. The potential exposure to franchise or enterprise value is manageable and commensurate with the volume and type of business conducted. Management adequately responds to changes of a market, technological or regulatory nature that affect the institution's reputation in the marketplace. Management has a good record of self-policing and correcting problems. Any deficiencies in MIS are minor. Administration procedures and processes are satisfactory. The bank has avoided conflicts of interest and other legal or control breaches. Risk management processes, internal control, and audits are generally effective. Management understands privacy issues and uses consumer information responsibly, although some exceptions may be noted.

- **High** — Vulnerability to changes in market and public perception is material in light of significant litigation, large losses, substantive violations of laws and regulations, or persistent customer dissatisfaction. The potential exposure to franchise or enterprise value may be increased by the number and type of accounts, the volume of assets under management, or the number of affected transactions. Management does not anticipate or take timely or appropriate actions in response to changes of a market, technological or regulatory nature. Weaknesses may be observed in one or more critical operational, administrative, or investment activities. The institution's performance in self-policing risk is suspect. Management has either not initiated, or has a poor record of, corrective action to address problems. Management information at various levels of the organization may exhibit significant weaknesses. Poor administration, conflicts of interest, and other legal or control breaches may be evident. Risk management processes, internal control, or audit may be less than effective in reducing exposure. Management is not aware of significant privacy issues or sometimes uses consumer information irresponsibly.

Credit Risk

Credit risk is the risk to current or anticipated earnings or capital arising from an obligor's failure to meet the terms of any contract with the bank or otherwise perform as agreed. Credit risk is found in all activities in which settlement or repayment depends on counterparty, issuer, or borrower performance. It exists any time bank funds are extended, committed, invested, or otherwise exposed through actual or implied contractual agreements, whether reflected on or off the balance sheet. (Updated 5/06/2013)

Credit risk is the most recognizable risk associated with banking. This risk, however, encompasses more than lending. Credit risk is present in a broad range of other bank activities, such as selecting investment portfolio products, derivatives trading partners, or foreign exchange counterparties. Credit risk also arises from country or sovereign exposure as well as indirectly through guarantor performance. (Updated 5/06/2013)

Summary Conclusions

Conclusions from the core assessment allow examiners to assess the quantity of credit risk, quality of credit risk management, aggregate credit risk, and the direction of risk.

Examiners consider both the quantity of credit risk and quality of credit risk management to derive the following conclusions.

Aggregate credit risk is:

☐ Low	☐ Moderate	☐ High

The direction of risk is expected to be:

☐ Decreasing	☐ Stable	☐ Increasing

Quantity of Credit Risk

Examiners use the following definitions to determine the quantity of credit risk. It is not necessary to meet every qualifier to be accorded a specific assessment.

The quantity of credit risk is:

☐ Low	☐ Moderate	☐ High

- **Low** — Current or prospective exposure to loss of earnings or capital is minimal. Credit exposures reflect conservative risk selection, underwriting and structures. The volume of substantive exceptions or overrides to the conservative underwriting standards poses minimal risk. Exposures represent a well- diversified distribution by investment grade (or equivalently strong nonrated borrowers) and borrower leverage. Borrowers operate in stable markets and industries. Risk of loss from concentrations is minimal. Limited sensitivity exists due to deteriorating economic, industry, competitive, regulatory, and technological factors. The bank's compensation is adequate to justify the risk being assumed. Portfolio growth presents no concerns and new products and marketing initiatives are conservative. Re-aging, extension, renewal, and refinancing practices are sound and pose no increased risk. The volume of troubled credits is low relative to capital and can be resolved in the normal course of business. Credit-related losses do not meaningfully affect current reserves and result in modest provisions relative to earnings.

- **Moderate** — Current or prospective exposure to loss of earnings or capital does not materially affect financial condition. Credit exposures reflect acceptable risk selection, underwriting and structures. Substantive exceptions or overrides to the sound underwriting standards may exist, but do not pose advanced risk. Exposures may include noninvestment grade (or equivalently strong nonrated borrowers) or leveraged borrowers, but borrowers typically operate in less volatile markets and industries. Exposure does not reflect significant concentrations. Vulnerability may exist due to deteriorating economic, industry, competitive, regulatory, and technological factors. The bank's compensation is adequate to justify the risk being assumed. While advanced portfolio growth may exist within specific products or sectors, it is in accordance with a reasonable plan. New credit products are reasonable. Re-aging, extension, renewal, and refinancing practices are satisfactory. The volume of troubled credits does not pose undue risk relative to capital and can be resolved within realistic time frames. Credit-related losses do not seriously deplete current reserves or necessitate large provisions relative to earnings.

- **High** — Current or prospective exposure to loss of earnings or capital is material. Credit exposures reflect aggressive risk selection, underwriting and structures. A large volume of substantive exceptions or overrides to sound underwriting standards exists. Exposures are skewed toward noninvestment grade (or equivalently strong nonrated borrowers) or highly leveraged borrowers, or borrowers operating in volatile markets and industries. Exposure reflects significant concentrations. Significant vulnerability exists due to deteriorating economic, industry, competitive, regulatory, and technological factors. The bank's compensation is inadequate to justify the risk being assumed. Portfolio growth, including products or sectors within the portfolio, is aggressive. New products are aggressive and often not sufficiently tested or planned for. Re-aging, extension, renewal, and refinancing practices are immoderate. The volume of troubled credits may be large relative to capital and may require an extended time to resolve. Credit-related losses may seriously deplete current reserves or necessitate large provisions relative to earnings.

Quality of Credit Risk Management

Examiners use the following definitions to determine the quality of credit risk management. It is not necessary to meet every qualifier to be accorded a specific assessment.

The quality of credit risk management is:

☐ Strong	☐ Satisfactory	☐ Weak

- **Strong** — The credit policy function comprehensively defines risk tolerance, responsibilities, and accountabilities. All aspects of credit policies are effectively communicated. The credit culture, including compensation, strikes an appropriate balance between marketing and credit considerations. New products and initiatives are fully researched, tested and approved before implementation. The credit granting process is extensively defined, well understood, and adhered to consistently. Credit analysis is thorough and timely. Risk measurement and monitoring systems are comprehensive and allow management to implement appropriate actions in response to changes in asset quality and market conditions. Information processes (manual and/or automated) are fully appropriate for the volume and complexity of activity. Any weaknesses are minor, with potential for nominal effect on earnings or capital. MIS produced by these information processes are accurate, timely, and complete, providing relevant information necessary for sound management decisions. Credit administration is effective. Management is effective and actively identifies and manages portfolio risk, including the risk relating to credit structure, policy exceptions, and concentrations. The ALLL methodology is well-defined, objective and clearly supports adequacy of current reserve levels. Personnel possess extensive technical and managerial expertise. Internal control is comprehensive and effective. The stature, quality, and independence of internal loan review and audit support highly effective control systems.

- **Satisfactory** — The credit policy function satisfactorily defines risk tolerance, responsibilities, and accountabilities. Key aspects of credit policies are effectively communicated. New products and initiatives are sometimes launched without sufficient research and testing. The credit culture, including compensation, appropriately balances marketing and credit considerations. The credit granting process is well-defined and understood. Credit analysis is adequate. Risk measurement and monitoring systems permit management to capably respond to changes in asset quality or market conditions. Information processes (manual and/or automated) are adequate for the volume and complexity of activity. MIS produced by these processes may require modest improvement in accuracy, timeliness, completeness, or relevance. Weaknesses in information processes (including resulting MIS) are not so significant that they lead management to decisions that materially affect earnings or capital. Internal grading and reporting accurately stratifies portfolio quality. Credit administration is adequate. Management adequately identifies and monitors portfolio risk, including the risk relating to credit structure and policy exceptions. Management's attention to credit risk diversification is adequate. The ALLL methodology is satisfactory and results in sufficient coverage of inherent credit losses. Personnel possess requisite technical and managerial expertise. Key internal controls are in place and effective. The stature, quality, and independence of internal loan review and audit are appropriate.

- **Weak** — The credit policy function may not effectively define risk tolerance, responsibilities, and accountabilities. Credit policies are not effectively communicated. New products and initiatives are often launched without sufficient research, testing, and risk analysis. The credit culture, including compensation, overemphasizes marketing relative to credit considerations. The credit granting process is not well-defined or not well understood. Credit analysis is insufficient relative to the risk. Risk measurement and monitoring systems may not permit management to implement timely and appropriate actions in response to changes in asset quality or market conditions. Information processes (manual and/or automated) are inappropriate for the volume and complexity of activity. MIS produced by these processes are inaccurate, untimely, incomplete, or insufficient to make sound management decisions. Weaknesses in information processes (including resulting MIS) can lead management to decisions that materially affect earnings or capital. Internal grading and reporting of credit exposure does not accurately stratify the portfolio's quality. Credit administration is ineffective. Management is unable to identify and monitor portfolio risk, including the risk relating to credit structure and/or policy exceptions. Management's attention to credit risk diversification is inadequate. The ALLL methodology is flawed and may result in insufficient coverage of inherent credit losses. Personnel lack requisite technical and managerial expertise. Key internal controls may be absent or ineffective. The stature, quality, or independence of internal loan review and/or audit is lacking.

Interest Rate Risk

Interest rate risk is the risk to current or anticipated earnings or capital arising from movements in interest rates. Interest rate risk results from differences between the timing of rate changes and the timing of cash flows (repricing risk); from changing rate relationships among different yield curves affecting bank activities (basis risk); from changing rate relationships across the spectrum of maturities (yield curve risk); and from interest-related options embedded in bank products (options risk). (Updated 5/06/2013)

The assessment of interest rate risk should consider risk from both an accounting perspective (i.e., the effect on the bank's accrual earnings) and an economic perspective (i.e., the effect on the market value of the bank's portfolio equity). In some banks, interest rate risk is included in the broader category of market risk. In contrast with price risk, which focuses on the mark-to-market portfolios (e.g., trading accounts), interest rate risk focuses on the value implications for accrual portfolios (e.g., held-to-maturity and available-for-sale accounts). (Updated 5/06/2013)

Summary Conclusions

Conclusions from the core assessment allow examiners to assess the quantity of interest rate risk, quality of interest rate risk management, aggregate interest rate risk, and the direction of risk.

Examiners consider both the quantity of interest rate risk and quality of interest rate risk management to derive the following conclusions.

Aggregate interest rate risk is:

☐ Low	☐ Moderate	☐ High

The direction of risk is expected to be:

☐ Decreasing	☐ Stable	☐ Increasing

Quantity of Interest Rate Risk

Examiners use the following definitions to determine the quantity of interest rate risk. It is not necessary to meet every qualifier to be accorded a specific assessment.

The quantity of interest rate risk is:

☐ Low	☐ Moderate	☐ High

- **Low** — Exposure reflects minimal repricing, basis, yield curve, and options risk. Positions used to manage interest rate risk exposure are well correlated to underlying risks. No significant mismatches on longer-term positions exist. The current or future volatility of earnings and capital is relatively insensitive to changes in interest rates or the exercise of options. Interest rate movements will have minimal adverse effect on the earnings and capital of the bank.

- **Moderate** — Exposure reflects manageable repricing, basis, yield curve, and options risk. Positions used to manage interest rate risk exposure are somewhat correlated. Mismatches on longer-term positions exist but are managed. The volatility in earnings or capital is not significantly affected by changes in interest rates or the exercise of options. Interest rate movements will not have a significant adverse effect on the earnings and capital of the bank.

- **High** — Exposure reflects significant repricing, basis, yield curve, or options risk. Positions used to manage interest rate risk exposure are poorly correlated. Significant mismatches on longer-term positions exist. Current or future volatility in earnings or capital due to changes in interest rates or the exercise of options is substantial. Interest rate movements could have a significant adverse effect on the earnings and capital of the bank.

Quality of Interest Rate Risk Management

Examiners use the following definitions to determine the quality of interest rate risk management. It is not necessary to meet every qualifier to be accorded a specific assessment.

The quality of interest rate risk management is:

☐ Strong	☐ Satisfactory	☐ Weak

- **Strong** — Policies are sound and effectively communicate guidelines for management of interest rate risk, including responsibilities, risk tolerance, and limits. Management fully understands all aspects of interest rate risk management from the earnings and economic perspectives, as appropriate. Discretionary risk positions are effectively measured and controlled. Management anticipates and quickly responds to changes in market conditions. Interest rate risk is well-understood at all appropriate levels of the organization. The interest rate risk management process is effective and prospective. Information processes (manual and/or automated) are fully appropriate for the volume and complexity of activity. Any weaknesses are minor, with potential for nominal effect on earnings or capital. MIS produced by these information processes are accurate, timely, and complete, with relevant information necessary for sound management decisions. Limit structures provide clear parameters for risk to earnings and capital under normal and adverse scenarios. The design and supporting technology of risk measurement tools, including models, are fully appropriate for the size and complexity of activity. Assumptions, software logic, and data input are documented, and independently validated and tested to ensure the measurement tools can accurately measure risks. Staff responsible for measuring exposures and monitoring risk limits is independent from staff executing risk-taking decisions.

- **Satisfactory** — Policies are generally sound and adequately communicate guidelines for management of interest rate risk, although minor weaknesses may be evident.

Management reasonably understands the key aspects of interest rate risk management from the earnings and economic perspectives, as appropriate. Discretionary risk positions are properly measured and controlled. Management adequately responds to changes in market conditions. Knowledge of interest rate risk exists at appropriate levels throughout the organization. The interest rate risk management process is adequate. Information processes (manual and/or automated) are adequate for the volume and complexity of activity. MIS produced by these processes may contain weaknesses in accuracy, timeliness, completeness, or relevance. Weaknesses in information processes (including resulting MIS) are not so significant that they lead management to decisions that materially affect earnings or capital. Limit structures are reasonable and sufficient to control the risk to earnings and capital under normal and adverse interest rate scenarios. The design and supporting technology of risk measurement tools, including models, are adequate for the size and complexity of activity. Assumptions, software logic and data input are documented, and independently validated and tested, but the measurement tools provide only a reasonable approximation of risks. Weaknesses are not so significant that they lead management to decisions that materially affect earnings or capital. Staff responsible for measuring exposures and monitoring risk is independent from staff executing risk-taking decisions.

- **Weak** — Policies are inadequate in communicating guidelines for management of interest rate risk. Management may not satisfactorily understand interest rate risk management from the earnings or economic perspective. Discretionary risk positions are not adequately measured or controlled. Management does not take timely or appropriate actions in response to changes in market conditions. Knowledge of interest rate risk may be lacking at appropriate management levels throughout the organization. The interest rate risk management process is deficient, given the relative size and complexity of the bank's on- and off-balance-sheet exposures. Information processes (manual and/or automated) are inappropriate for the volume and complexity of activity. MIS produced by these processes are inaccurate, untimely, incomplete, or insufficient to make sound management decisions. Weaknesses in information processes (including resulting MIS) can lead management to decisions that materially affect earnings or capital. Limit structures are not reasonable, or do not reflect an understanding of the risks to earnings and capital under normal and adverse scenarios. The design and supporting technology of risk measurement tools, including models, are inappropriate for the size and complexity of activity. Risk measurement validation or testing is either not performed or seriously flawed. Risks are inaccurately measured, impairing the ability of management to make sound decisions. The potential effect on earnings or capital can be material. Staff responsible for measuring exposures and monitoring risk is not independent from staff executing risk-taking decisions.

Liquidity Risk

Liquidity risk is the risk to current or anticipated earnings or capital arising from an inability to meet obligations when they come due. Liquidity risk includes the inability to access funding sources or manage fluctuations in funding levels. Liquidity risk also results from a bank's failure to recognize or address changes in market conditions that affect its ability to liquidate assets quickly and with minimal loss in value. (Updated 5/06/2013)

Liquidity risk, like credit risk, is a recognizable risk associated with banking. The nature of liquidity risk, however, has changed in recent years. Increased investment alternatives for retail depositors, sophisticated off-balance-sheet products with complicated cash-flow implications, and a general increase in the credit sensitivity of bank customers are all examples of factors that complicate liquidity risk. (Updated 5/06/2013)

Summary Conclusions

Conclusions from the core assessment allow examiners to assess the quantity of liquidity risk, quality of liquidity risk management, aggregate liquidity risk, and the direction of risk.

Examiners consider both the quantity of liquidity risk and quality of liquidity risk management to derive the following conclusions.

Aggregate liquidity risk is:

☐ Low	☐ Moderate	☐ High

The direction of risk is expected to be:

☐ Decreasing	☐ Stable	☐ Increasing

Quantity of Liquidity Risk

Examiners use the following definitions to determine the quantity of liquidity risk. It is not necessary to meet every qualifier to be accorded a specific assessment.

The quantity of liquidity risk is:

☐ Low	☐ Moderate	☐ High

- **Low** — The bank is not vulnerable to funding difficulties should a material adverse change in market perception occur. Earnings and capital exposure from the liquidity risk profile is negligible. Sources of deposits and borrowings are widely diversified, with no material concentrations. Ample funding sources and structural cash flow symmetry exist in all tenors. Stable deposits and a strong market acceptance of the bank's name offers the bank a competitive liability cost advantage. Management has identified reasonable alternatives to credit-sensitive funding, if relied upon, and can easily implement the alternatives with no disruption in strategic lines of business.

- **Moderate** — The bank is not excessively vulnerable to funding difficulties should a material adverse change in market perception occur. Earnings or capital exposure from the liquidity risk profile is manageable. Sources of funding are reasonably diverse but minor concentrations may exist, and funds providers may be moderately credit sensitive. Some groups of providers may share common investment objectives or be subject to similar economic influences. Sufficient funding sources, and structural balance sheet and cash flow symmetry exist to provide stable, cost-effective liquidity in most environments, without significant disruption in strategic lines of business.

- **High** — The bank's liquidity profile makes it vulnerable to funding difficulties should a material adverse change occur. Significant concentrations of funding may exist, or there may be a significant volume of providers that are highly credit-sensitive. Large funds providers may share common investment objectives or be subject to similar economic influences. The bank may currently, or potentially, experience market resistance, which could affect its ability to access needed funds at a reasonable cost. There may be an increasing demand for liquidity with declining medium- and long-term alternatives. Funding sources and balance sheet structures may currently result in, or suggest, potential difficulty in sustaining long-term liquidity on a cost-effective basis. Potential exposure to loss of earnings or capital due to high liability costs or unplanned asset reduction may be substantial. Liquidity needs may trigger the necessity for funding alternatives under a contingency funding plan, including the sale of, or disruption in, a strategic line of business.

Quality of Liquidity Risk Management

Examiners use the following definitions to determine the quality of liquidity risk management. It is not necessary to meet every qualifier to be accorded a specific assessment.

The quality of liquidity risk management is:

☐ Strong	☐ Satisfactory	☐ Weak

- **Strong** — Management incorporates all key aspects of liquidity risk into its overall risk management process, and anticipates and responds promptly to changing market conditions. There are clearly articulated policies that provide clear insight and guidance on appropriate risk-taking and management. Information processes (manual and/or automated) are fully appropriate for the volume and complexity of activity. Any weaknesses are minor, with potential for nominal effect on earnings or capital. MIS produced by these information processes are accurate, timely, and complete, with relevant information necessary for sound management decisions. Liquidity planning is fully integrated with strategic planning, budgeting, and financial management processes. Management gives appropriate attention to managing balance sheet symmetry, cash flows, cost effectiveness, and evaluating liquidity alternatives. A comprehensive contingency funding plan exists which is fully integrated into overall risk management processes, and which will enable the bank to respond to potential crisis situations in a timely manner and to the fullest capacity of the bank.

- **Satisfactory** — Management incorporates most of the key aspects of liquidity risk into its overall risk management process. Management adequately responds to changes in market conditions. Liquidity risk management policies and practices are adequate, although there may be some short falls. Liquidity planning is integrated with the strategic planning, budgeting, and financial management processes. Information processes (manual and/or automated) are adequate for the volume and complexity of activity. MIS produced by these processes may contain weaknesses in accuracy, timeliness, completeness, or relevance. Weaknesses in information processes (including resulting MIS) are not so significant that they lead management to decisions that materially affect earnings or capital. Management realistically assesses the funding markets and pays sufficient attention to diversification. Management attention to balance sheet symmetry, cash flow, and cost effectiveness is generally appropriate. Management has a satisfactory contingency funding plan to manage liquidity risk and is generally prepared to manage potential crisis situations.

- **Weak** — Management does not satisfactorily address key aspects of liquidity risk. Management is not anticipating or implementing timely or appropriate actions in response to changes in market conditions. Polices are inadequate or incomplete, deficient in one or more material respects. Liquidity planning is not sufficiently integrated in the strategic planning, budgeting, and financial management processes. Information processes (manual and/or automated) are inappropriate for the volume and complexity of activity. MIS produced by these processes are inaccurate, untimely, incomplete, or insufficient to make sound management decisions. Weaknesses in information processes (including resulting MIS) can lead management to decisions that materially affect earnings or capital. Management has not realistically assessed the bank's access to the funding markets, has paid insufficient attention to diversification, or has limited awareness of large funds providers and their sensitivity. Management attention to balance sheet and cash flow symmetry is inadequate. The contingency planning process is deficient, inhibiting management's ability to minimize liquidity problems in a deteriorating scenario or to manage potential crisis situations. Management's evaluation of liquidity alternatives does not adequately consider cost effectiveness or the availability of these alternatives in a variety of market environments.

Price Risk

Price risk is the risk to current or anticipated earnings or capital arising from changes in the value of either trading portfolios or other obligations that are entered into as part of distributing risk. These portfolios typically are subject to daily price movements and are accounted for primarily on a mark-to-market basis. This risk occurs most significantly from market-making, dealing, and position-taking in interest rate, foreign exchange, equity, commodities, and credit markets. (Updated 5/06/2013)

Price risk also arises from bank activities whose value changes are reflected in the income statement, such as in lending pipelines, other real estate owned, and mortgage servicing rights. The risk to earnings or capital resulting from the conversion of a bank's financial statements from foreign currency translation also should be assessed under price risk. As with interest rate risk, many banks include price risk in the broader category of market risk. (Updated 5/06/2013)

Summary Conclusions

Conclusions from the core assessment allow examiners to assess the quantity of price risk, quality of price risk management, aggregate price risk, and the direction of risk.

Examiners consider both the quantity of price risk and quality of price risk management to derive the following conclusions.

Aggregate price risk is:

☐ Low	☐ Moderate	☐ High

The direction of risk is expected to be:

☐ Decreasing	☐ Stable	☐ Increasing

Quantity of Price Risk

Examiners use the following definitions to determine the quantity of price risk. It is not necessary to meet every qualifier to be accorded a specific assessment.

The quantity of price risk is:

☐ Low	☐ Moderate	☐ High

- **Low** — Exposure reflects limited open or illiquid price risk positions. As a result, earnings and capital are not vulnerable to significant loss. Exposure, whether arising from proprietary or customer-driven transactions, involves liquid and readily manageable products, markets, and levels of activity. The bank has a low volume of assets and liabilities that are accounted for at fair value through earnings (e.g., lending pipelines and mortgage servicing rights). If exposures to foreign currency translation exist, the translation adjustments will have an immaterial effect on earnings, capital, or capital ratios.

- **Moderate** — Exposure, whether arising from speculative or customer- driven transactions, reflects moderate open or illiquid price risk positions, limiting the potential for significant loss to earnings and capital. As such, earnings and capital have moderate vulnerability to volatility from revaluation requirements. The bank has access to a variety of risk management instruments and markets at reasonable costs, given the size, tenor and complexity of open positions. Assets and liabilities that are accounted for at fair value (e.g., lending pipelines and mortgage servicing rights) are unlikely to materially affect earnings and capital. If exposures to foreign currency translation exist, the translation adjustments are not expected to have an adverse effect on earnings, capital, or capital ratios.

- **High** — Exposure reflects significant open or illiquid price risk positions, exposing the bank to a significant loss of earnings and capital. Exposure may arise from transactions or positions that are taken as a result of management or trader views of the market, in conjunction with customer transactions, or from market-making activities. Exposures may be difficult or costly to close out or hedge due to size, complexity, or generally illiquid markets, tenors, or products. A significant volume of assets and liabilities are accounted for at fair value (e.g., lending pipelines and mortgage servicing rights), and valuation changes have the potential to materially affect earnings and capital. If exposures to foreign currency translation exist, the translation adjustments could have a material adverse effect on earnings, capital, or capital ratios.

Quality of Price Risk Management

Examiners use the following definitions to determine the quality of price risk management. It is not necessary to meet every qualifier to be accorded a specific assessment.

The quality of price risk management is:

☐ Strong	☐ Sastisfactory	☐ Weak

- **Strong** — Approved policies reflect the bank's risk appetite, provide clear authorities and responsibilities, and delineate appropriate limits. Management fully understands price risk and actively monitors products, market trends, and changes in market conditions. Information processes (manual and/or automated) are fully appropriate for the volume and complexity of activity. Any weaknesses are minor, with potential for nominal effect on earnings or capital. MIS produced by these information processes are accurate, timely, and complete, with relevant information necessary for sound management decisions. Models and methodologies are independently validated, tested, and documented. There is a sound independent valuation process for all significant positions. Management fully researches and documents the risk of new product initiatives prior to implementation. Limit structures are reasonable, clear, and effectively communicated. The limits also reflect a clear understanding of the risk to earnings and capital under normal and adverse scenarios. Staff responsible for measuring and monitoring price risk is well-qualified and independent from risk-taking activities. Management has a rigorous program for stress testing positions. If exposures to foreign currency translation exist, management fully understands all aspects of the risk.

- **Satisfactory** — Approved policies provide generally clear authorities, reasonable limits, and assignment of responsibilities. Management understands the key aspects of price risk. Management adequately responds to changes in market conditions. Price risk management processes address major exposures. Information processes (manual and/or automated) are adequate for the volume and complexity of activity. MIS produced by these processes may contain weaknesses in accuracy, timeliness, completeness, or relevance. Weaknesses in information processes (including resulting MIS) are not so significant that they lead management to decisions that materially affect earnings or capital. Risk measurement tools and methods may have minor deficiencies or weaknesses, but are sufficient, given the size and complexity of activities. Models and methodologies are validated and acceptable. Positions are independently valued. Management considers the risk of new product initiatives prior to implementation. Limit structures are reasonable, clear, and effectively communicated. Limits also reflect an understanding of the risk to earnings and capital under normal and adverse scenarios. Staff responsible for measuring and monitoring price risk is qualified and independent from risk-taking activities. Processes for stress testing positions are generally adequate. If exposures to foreign currency translation exist, management understands the key aspects of the risk.

- **Weak** — Management does not satisfactorily address key aspects of price risk and the underlying policies may have significant weaknesses. Management is not implementing timely or appropriate actions in response to changes in market conditions. Knowledge of price risk may be lacking at appropriate management levels throughout the organization. The price risk management process is deficient in one or more of the following ways. Risk measurement tools and methods are inadequate given the size and complexity of activities. Processes (manual and/or automated) are inappropriate for the volume and complexity of activity. MIS produced by these processes are inaccurate, untimely, incomplete, or insufficient to make sound management decisions. Weaknesses in information processes (including resulting MIS) can lead management to decisions that materially affect earnings or capital. Position valuations are performed infrequently, exclude major products, or may not be sufficiently independent. Management does not adequately consider the risk of new product initiatives prior to implementation. Limit structures may not be reasonable, clear, or effectively communicated. Limits also may not reflect a complete understanding of the risk to earnings and capital. Staff responsible for measuring and monitoring price risk is not independent of risk-taking activities. The bank does not have a formal program to stress test positions. If exposures to foreign currency translation exist, management does not satisfactorily address key aspects of the risk.

Operational Risk

Operational risk is the risk to current or anticipated earnings or capital arising from inadequate or failed internal processes or systems, human errors or misconduct, or adverse external events. Operational losses result from internal fraud; external fraud; inadequate or inappropriate employment practices and workplace safety; failure to meet professional obligations involving clients, products, and business practices; damage to physical assets; business disruption and systems failures; and failures in execution, delivery, and process management. Operational losses do not include opportunity costs, forgone revenue, or costs related to risk management and control enhancements implemented to prevent future operational losses. (Updated 5/06/2013)

The quantity of operational risk and the quality of operational risk management are heavily influenced by the quality and effectiveness of a bank's system of internal control. The quality of the audit function, although independent of operational risk management, also is a key assessment factor. Audit can affect the operating performance of a bank by helping to identify and ensure correction of weaknesses in risk management or controls. The quality of due diligence and business continuity planning are other key assessment factors for mitigating operational risk arising from third-party relationships and events outside a bank's direct control, such as natural disasters and damage to or loss of critical infrastructure. (Updated 5/06/2013)

Summary Conclusions

Conclusions from the core assessment allow examiners to assess the quantity of operational risk, quality of operational risk management, aggregate operational risk, and the direction of risk.

Examiners consider both the quantity of operational risk and quality of operational risk management to derive the following conclusions.

Aggregate operational risk is:

☐ Low	☐ Moderate	☐ High

The direction of risk is expected to be:

☐ Decreasing	☐ Stable	☐ Increasing

Quantity of Operational Risk

Examiners use the following definitions to determine the quantity of operational risk. It is not necessary to meet every qualifier to be accorded a specific assessment.

The quantity of operational risk is:

☐ Low	☐ Moderate	☐ High

- **Low** — Operational loss events and control failures are expected to have little effect on earnings or capital. The complexity of products and services, the volume of transaction processing, and the state of internal systems expose the bank to minimal risk from fraud, errors, execution issues, or processing disruptions. The risks related to new products, outsourcing, accounting issues, technology changes, bank acquisitions or divestitures, and external threats are minimal and well-understood. Process and control breakdowns and exceptions to risk tolerances and limits are rare.

- **Moderate** — Operational loss events and control failures are expected to have a marginal effect on earnings or capital. The complexity of products and services, the volume of transaction processing, and the state of internal systems expose the bank to increased risks from fraud, errors, execution issues, or processing disruptions. The risks related to new products, outsourcing, accounting issues, technology changes, bank acquisitions or divestitures, and external threats are manageable. Process and control breakdowns and exceptions to risk tolerances and limits are increasing.

- **High** — Operational loss events and control failures are expected to have a significant effect on earnings or capital and could result from one significant loss or multiple important losses. The complexity of products and services, the volume of transaction processing, and the state of internal systems expose the bank to significant risks from fraud, errors, execution issues, or processing disruptions. The risks related to new products, outsourcing, accounting issues, technology changes, bank acquisitions or divestitures, and external threats are substantial and may not have been fully analyzed. Process and control breakdowns and exceptions to risk tolerances and limits may be of significant concern.

Quality of Operational Risk Management

Examiners use the following definitions to determine the quality of operational risk management. It is not necessary to meet every qualifier to be accorded a specific assessment.

The quality of operational risk management is:

☐ Strong	☐ Sastisfactory	☐ Weak

- **Strong** — Management anticipates and responds to key aspects of risk associated with operational changes, systems development, emerging technologies, and external threats. Management effectively analyzes risks and develops robust operating processes, internal controls, and audit coverage, which are consistently applied across the organization. Management has developed appropriate tools to identify key risks and processes to determine how those risks will be managed (e.g., accept the risk, institute a corresponding control, and/or hedge against the risk). Systems are in place to respond to new and emerging products, evolving technologies, changes in strategic direction, and fundamental shifts in external factors. There are strong governance and staffing processes in place covering the corporate function, the lines of business, and the functional areas. Management comprehensively plans for continuity and reliability of service, including services provided by third-parties. There is an effective and thorough monitoring and control system in place governing operations and activities that have been outsourced or moved offshore. Appropriate processes and controls exist to manage data and protect it from unauthorized change or disclosure. Management has appropriate MIS, which is regularly provided to senior management and other key stakeholders, that addresses key operational risks and includes risk metrics, trends, and action items.

- **Satisfactory** — Management satisfactorily responds to risks associated with operational changes, systems development, emerging technologies, and external threats. Management generally analyzes risks and develops adequate operating processes, internal controls, and audit coverage, which are usually applied across the organization. Management has developed appropriate tools to identify most key risks and processes to determine how those risks will be managed (e.g., accept the risk, institute a corresponding control, and/or hedge against the risk), although these tools may need further enhancement. Systems are in place to respond to new and emerging products, evolving technologies, changes in strategic direction, and fundamental shifts in external factors. There are adequate governance and staffing processes in place covering the corporate function, the lines of business, and the functional areas. Management adequately plans for continuity and reliability of significant services, including services provided by third-parties. There is an adequate monitoring and control system in place over operations and activities that have been outsourced or moved offshore. Processes and controls to manage data and protect it from unauthorized change or disclosure are adequate. Management has MIS on operational risk, which may have minor deficiencies. Management has generally adequate MIS, which is regularly provided to senior management and other key stakeholders, that addresses operational risks. This MIS may have minor weakness, such as the lack of fully developed or identified risk metrics, trends, and action items.

- **Weak** — Management may not take timely and appropriate actions to respond to operational changes, systems development, emerging technologies, and external threats. Management does not properly analyze risks and has insufficient operating processes, internal controls, and audit coverage in some or all areas of the organization. There may be tools in place to identify some key risks, but these tools may be deficient. Processes to determine how to manage identified risks are poorly designed. The systems in place, if any, to respond to new and emerging products, emerging technologies, changes in strategic direction, and fundamental shifts in external factors have weaknesses. Governance and staffing processes may not be well-defined and clear responsibility for operational risk management across the organization may not be clearly established and developed. Management has not sufficiently planned for continuity and reliability of services. The monitoring and control system in place over operations and activities that have been outsourced or moved offshore is inadequate or incomplete. Processes and controls to manage data and protect it from unauthorized change or disclosure are deficient or nonexistent. MIS is inadequate and senior management reporting is not well-established. MIS does not provide a clear assessment of operational risk and risk metrics, trends, and action items are not identified or developed.

Compliance Risk

Compliance risk is the risk to current or anticipated earnings or capital arising from violations of laws, rules, or regulations, or from nonconformance with prescribed practices, internal policies and procedures, or ethical standards. This risk exposes a bank to fines, civil money penalties, payment of damages, and the voiding of contracts. Compliance risk can result in diminished reputation, reduced franchise or enterprise value, limited business opportunities, and lessened expansion potential. (Updated 5/06/2013)

Compliance risk is not limited to risk from failure to comply with consumer protection laws; it encompasses the risk of noncompliance with *all* laws and regulations, as well as prudent ethical standards and contractual obligations. It also includes the exposure to litigation (known as legal risk) from all aspects of banking, traditional and nontraditional. (Updated 5/06/2013)

Summary Conclusions

Conclusions from the core assessment allow examiners to assess the quantity of compliance risk, quality of compliance risk management, aggregate compliance risk, and the direction of risk.

Examiners consider both the quantity of compliance risk and quality of compliance risk management to derive the following conclusions.

Aggregate compliance risk is:

☐ Low	☐ Moderate	☐ High

The direction of risk is expected to be:

☐ Decreasing	☐ Stable	☐ Increasing

Quantity of Compliance Risk

Examiners use the following definitions to determine the quantity of compliance risk. It is not necessary to meet every qualifier to be accorded a specific assessment.

The quantity of compliance risk is:

☐ Low	☐ Moderate	☐ High

- **Low** — The nature and extent of business activities limit the company's potential exposure to violations or noncompliance. The bank has few violations and management quickly and adequately addresses violations when uncovered with no effect on reputation, capital, earnings or business opportunity. The bank's history of complaints or litigation is good.

- **Moderate** — The nature and extent of business activities may increase the potential for violations or noncompliance. The bank may have violations outstanding which are correctable in the normal course of business with little effect on reputation, capital, earnings, or business opportunity. The bank's history of complaints or litigation is not a concern.

- **High** — The nature and extent of business activities significantly increase the potential for serious or frequent violations or noncompliance. The bank may have substantive violations outstanding that could affect reputation, capital, earnings, or business opportunity. The bank may have a history of serious complaints or litigation.

Quality of Compliance Risk Management

Examiners use the following definitions to determine the quality of compliance risk management. It is not necessary to meet every qualifier to be accorded a specific assessment.

The quality of compliance risk management is:

☐ Strong	☐ Satisfactory	☐ Weak

- **Strong** — Management demonstrates a high commitment and concern for all compliance issues. Management anticipates and addresses key aspects of compliance risk. Management takes timely and effective actions in response to compliance issues or regulatory changes. Compliance risk management systems, transaction and surveillance monitoring systems, and information processes are sound and the bank has a strong control culture, which has proven effective. Management provides substantial resources and has established accountability and timely enforced it for compliance performance. Compliance considerations are an integral part of product or system developments. Compliance training programs are effective. Technology is effectively used to identify compliance violations and nonconformance at the point of transaction as well as post transaction. (Updated 9/28/2012)

- **Satisfactory** — Management demonstrates a reasonable commitment and concern for all compliance issues. Management addresses key aspects of compliance risk. Management takes appropriate actions in response to compliance issues or regulatory changes. Compliance risk management systems, transaction and surveillance monitoring systems, and information processes are adequate to avoid significant or frequent violations or noncompliance. Management has established or enforced accountability for compliance performance and corrects problems in the normal course of business. Compliance considerations are incorporated into product or system developments. Management provides adequate resources and training given the complexity of products and operations. Management understands and has adequately addressed consumer privacy issues. Technology or internal control is adequate to manage compliance at inception. (Updated 9/28/2012)

- **Weak** — Management generally does not demonstrate a reasonable commitment and/or concern for all compliance issues. Management does not satisfactorily address key aspects of compliance risk. Management is not anticipating or implementing timely or appropriate actions in response to compliance issues or regulatory changes. Compliance risk management systems, transaction and surveillance monitoring systems, and information processes are deficient. Management has not provided adequate resources or training, and/or has not established or enforced accountability for compliance performance. Errors are often not detected internally, or corrective actions are often ineffective and not timely. Compliance considerations are not incorporated into product or system developments. Management has not adequately addressed the privacy of consumer records. Technology or internal control is not used or ineffectively used to identify violations or nonconformance. (Updated 9/28/2012)

Internal Control and Audit

Internal Control

Internal control is the systems, policies, procedures, and processes effected by the board of directors, management, and other personnel to safeguard bank assets, limit or control risks, and achieve a bank's objectives.

Summary Conclusion

Conclusions from the core assessment allow examiners to assess internal control.

The overall system of internal control is:

☐ Strong	☐ Satisfactory	☐ Weak

Examiners use the following definitions to assess internal control. It is not necessary to meet every qualifier to be accorded a specific assessment.

- **Strong** — The organization's strategic philosophy ascribes importance to a robust control environment and the board strongly supports that environment. The system of internal control provides for reliable financial reporting, segregation of duties, safeguarding of assets and information, and compliance with applicable laws and regulations. The organization has an effective process in place to ensure that controls as described in its policy and procedures manuals are operating effectively, and these controls are periodically reviewed through a self-assessment and an independent evaluation. Follow-up is required when internal and external auditors and regulatory agencies recommend improvements to the internal control system, and that follow-up is timely and appropriate.

- **Satisfactory** — The organization's strategic philosophy ascribes some importance to an adequate control environment, and the board supports that environment. The system of internal control generally provides for reliable financial reporting, segregation of duties, safeguarding of assets and information, and compliance with applicable laws and regulations. Controls can be implemented in areas found to have deficiencies. The organization has an adequate process in place to ensure that controls as described in its policy and procedures manuals are applied as they are meant to be applied. A periodic self-assessment or independent evaluation of internal controls may have minor deficiencies. The organization generally follows-up when internal and external auditors and regulatory agencies recommend improvements to the internal control system.

- **Weak** — The organization's strategic philosophy does not ascribe or otherwise sufficiently emphasize the importance to an adequate control environment, and the board provides marginal support for such an environment. The system of internal control does not completely provide for reliable financial reporting, segregation of duties, safeguarding of assets and information, and compliance with applicable laws and regulations. Controls can not easily be implemented in areas found to have deficiencies. The organization has an inadequate process to ensure that controls as described in its policy and procedures manuals are applied as they are meant to be applied. A periodic self-assessment or independent evaluation of internal controls may be lacking or have significant deficiencies. The organization's follow-up on identified control weaknesses is inadequate or lacks senior management commitment.

Audit

Audit programs provide objective, independent reviews and evaluations of bank activities, internal controls, compliance, and management information systems; help maintain or improve the effectiveness of bank risk management processes, controls, and corporate governance; and provide reasonable assurance that transactions are recorded accurately and in a timely manner and financial and regulatory reports are accurate and complete.

Summary Conclusion

Conclusions from the core assessment allow examiners to assess the audit program.

The overall audit program is:

☐ Strong	☐ Satisfactory	☐ Weak

Examiners use the following definitions to assess the audit program. It is not necessary to meet every qualifier to be accorded a specific assessment. Examiners consider the key attributes in the audit core assessment when assessing the audit program. These key attributes are normally present to distinguish between assessments, but examiners will need to factor in the bank's size, the nature of its activities, and its risk profile to arrive at an overall assessment. Examiners should also consider whether the audit program includes appropriate risk-based coverage of consumer protection and BSA/AML/OFAC compliance risk management systems. (Updated 9/28/2012)

- **Strong** — The audit program attains the highest level of respect and stature in the organization, which is continually confirmed by the attitudes, actions, and support of the board and management. Audit's role is independent, clearly spelled out, and incorporated into overall corporate risk management, new product and service deployment, changes in strategy and tactical plans, and organizational and structural changes.

- **Satisfactory** — The audit program attains an adequate level of respect and stature in the organization and is generally supported by the actions of the board and management. Audit's role in overall corporate risk management and participation in new product and service deployment, changes in strategy and tactical plans, and organizational and structural changes may be limited, but is conducted in accordance with its assigned responsibilities.

- **Weak** — The audit program does not carry sufficient stature given the organization's risk profile. The audit program does not have the full support of or appropriate oversight by the board and management. Audit's role is unclear and not incorporated into overall corporate risk management, new product and service deployment, changes in strategy and tactical plans, and organizational and structural changes.

Appendix

Appendix A: Aggregate Risk Matrix

QUALITY OF RISK MANAGEMENT	QUANTITY OF RISK		
	Low	Moderate	High
Weak	Low to Moderate	Moderate to High	High
Satisfactory	Low	Moderate	Moderate to High
Strong	Low	Low to Moderate	Moderate

This matrix is a guide to assessing aggregate risk. Aggregate risk is the level of supervisory concern, which is a summary judgment incorporating the assessments of the quantity of risk and the quality of risk management (examiners weigh the relative importance of each). The assessments on this matrix are guides only; examiners should feel free to consider other relevant factors not depicted on this matrix.

References

Regulations

12 CFR 28, International Banking Activities
12 CFR 30, Safety and Soundness Standards
12 CFR 363, Annual Independent Audits and Reporting Requirements

Comptroller's Handbook

"Bank Supervision Process"
"Community Bank Supervision"
"Compliance Management System"
"Federal Branches and Agencies Supervision"
"Internal and External Audits"
"Internal Control"
"Internal Control Questionnaires and Verification Procedures"
"Loan Portfolio Management"
"Related Organizations"

OCC Issuances

Banking Bulletin 93-38, "Interagency Examination Coordination Guidelines"
PPM 5400-8 (rev), "Supervision Work Papers"
PPM 5500-1 (rev), "Coordination with Foreign Supervisors"

FFIEC Publications

Bank Secrecy Act/Anti-Money Laundering Examination Manual
Information Technology Examination Handbook

Other

Basel Committee on Banking Supervision, "Core Principles for Effective Banking
    Supervision."
Committee of Sponsoring Organizations of the Treadway Commission (COSO), "Internal
    Control – Integrated Framework"